Vaiśeṣika-Sūtra
of
Kaṇāda

न्यायशास्त्रप्रशंसा

प्रदीपः सर्वविद्यानाम् उपायः सर्वकर्मणाम् ।
आश्रयः सर्वधर्माणाम् विद्योद्देशे प्रकीर्तिता ॥

Vaiśeṣika-Sūtra of Kaṇāda

by

Debasish Chakrabarty

DK PRINTWORLD
Publishers of Indian Traditions

Cataloging in Publication Data — DK
[Courtesy: D.K. Agencies (P) Ltd. <docinfo@dkagencies.com>]

Kaṇāda, author.
Vaiśeṣika-sūtra of Kaṇāda / [edited and translated] by Debasish Chakrabarty.
pages cm
English and Sanskrit (Sanskrit in Devanagari and roman).
"First published in India in 2003" – Title page verso.
Includes bibliographical references and index.
ISBN 9788124602294

1. Vaiśeṣika – Early works to 1800. 2. Kaṇāda. Vaiśeṣikasūtra. I. Chakrabarty, Debasish, 1973- editor, translator. II. Kaṇāda. Vaiśeṣikasūtra. III. Kaṇāda. Vaiśeṣikasūtra. English. IV. Title.

LCC B132.V2K36 2022 | DDC 181.44 23

ISBN: 978-81-246-0229-4
First published in India in 2003
Second impression in 2015
Third impression in 2022

Printed and published by:
D.K. Printworld (P) Ltd.
Regd. office : "Vedaśrī", F-395, Sudarshan Park
(ESI Metro Station) New Delhi – 110015
Phones : (011) 2545 3975; 2546 6019;
E-mail: indology@dkprintworld.com
Web: www.dkprintworld.com

Contents

Acknowledgements

This work would not have been possible without the help and support of the following:

PROF. KAPIL KAPOOR for making the Indian scholastic tradition come alive in class after class and for being a deep and abiding influence on the work.

The ŚĀSTRA GROUP at JNU for the sheer excitement with ideas.

BIKRAM MITRA, friend at NID, for the lovely cover.

L.C. MEHTA at L.D. Institute of Indology for permitting the reference and photography of the *Kiraṇāvali* and *Padārthadharma-saṁgraha* manuscripts.

Last but not the least, friend and wife PRIYANKA for surviving the myriad proof readings.

Debasish Chakrabarty

Dedicated

to

Prof. Kapil Kapoor

a little something for his bookshelf

The Śāstra Group at Jawaharlal Nehru University — An Introduction —

AT the Centre of Linguistics and English, Jawaharlal Nehru University, beginning in 1978, a conscious decision was taken to introduce courses in the Indian intellectual traditions in grammar, literary theory and philosophy so that the young post-graduates and research students who come to J.N.U., who are among the brightest minds in the country, are in a position to interact meaningfully with the Western thought and on level ground. This intellectual tradition, we know, had three main contending schools of thought — the Brahmin (also called the Grammarians), the Buddhist and the Jaina. The Brahmin School, the Grammarians, were divided into *āstika* (orthodox) and *nāstika* (heterodox) schools. These three traditions are enshrined mainly in Sanskrit and also in Pāli (Buddhist) and Prākr̥ta (Jaina). All the streams composed their major texts in Sanskrit which for more than 3000 years has continued to be the language of learning and scholarship in India. These three traditions, contrary to the popular perception, continue to be living traditions though through exigencies of history they have become relatively restricted to some traditional centres and institutes of learning. But the tradition is alive — this tradition of knowledge may be compared to a river, the *Gaṅgā pravāha,* which sometimes and/or at some places becomes narrow and elsewhere and at another time is a broad free flowing stream.

The task is to make this learning a part of the mainstream education, to establish a bridge between the wealth of scholarship in this tradition and the new centres of learning, the Indian universities. How is this to be achieved?

It can be achieved by making the seminal texts of the Indian intellectual traditions widely and inexpensively available. For this, we have

1. to prepare editions of seminal intellectual texts *in different scripts*,
2. to translate/re-translate the seminal texts into English and into major Indian languages (and into major European languages), and prepare careful modern translations in contemporary idiom,
3. to expound the important theoretical frameworks in a modern idiom to bring out their contemporary relevance.

In this perspective, and with this end in view, the Centre of Linguistics and English, Jawaharlal Nehru University, New Delhi, had introduced courses first in the Indian intellectual traditions in grammar, literary theory and philosophy and then courses in the seminal texts — the grammar of Pāṇini, *Aṣṭādhyāyī,* Bharata's *Nāṭyaśāstra,* Bhartṛhari's *Vākyapadīya* and Patañjali's *Yogasūtra. Aṣṭādhyāyī* is studied as a primary modelling device of knowledge; *Nāṭyaśāstra* is studied as a text of communication; *Vākyapadīya* is unrivalled as a text of philosophy of language; and, *Yogasūtra* is a text of cognition and cognitive processes. This, over the years, then led in due time to considerable expositional and comparative research by a growing body of brilliant young boys and girls who, with their minds engaged by the powerful texts, became deeply involved in and committed to the Indian traditions of thought and became convinced that the theoretical frameworks of this tradition can be meaningfully related to both the contemporary Indian realities and the modern Western thought.

These young scholars are a group devoted to the task of opening out the Indian thought by (i) translating the seminal texts, (ii) writing expository commentaries on those texts, and (iii) applying the Indian theoretical frameworks to modern Indian and Western texts to show the power, validity and in-built development potential of these frameworks. This group, called **The Śāstra Group,** at present has these founding members:

1. Ananya Vajpeyi
2. Anuradha Ghosh
3. Atanu Bhattacharya
4. Debasish Chakrabarty
5. Gaurhari Behera
6. Mayurika Chakravarti
7. Nabanita Banerjee
8. Nalini M. Ratnam
9. Nitoo Das
10. Dr. Rajnish Kumar Mishra
11. Dr. Sadhana Parashar
12. Dr. Saugata Bhaduri
13. Shankaranarayanan
14. Shruti Pant
15. Sunita Murmu
16. Dr. Sushant Kumar Mishra
17. Swati Mustafi
18. Simi Malhotra
19. Prof. Kapil Kapoor

Objectives of Śāstra Group

1. To prepare inexpensive script variants of principal intellectual texts in the major Indian scripts.
2. To prepare modern translations of these texts in major Indian languages and produce both inexpensive student editions of each and multilingual CD texts.
3. To apply the Indian theoretical frameworks contemporary Indian texts and texts of other cultures.
4. To explore the possibility of producing reference bibliography of Sanskrit studies around the globe.

5. To prepare multi-lingual glossaries of intellectual terms in grammar, literary theory and philosophy. and
6. To start a *Journal of Indic Studies.*

The following texts have been identified in the first instance:

I. Grammar and Phonetics

1. *Aṣṭādhyāyī*
2. *Vājasaneyi Prātiśākhya*
3. *Pāṇinīya Śikṣā*
4. 1st *Āhnika of Mahābhāṣya*

II. Literary Theory

5. Bharata's *Nāṭyaśāstra*
6. Bhāmaha's *Kāvyālaṅkāra*
7. Daṇḍin's *Kāvyādarśa*
8. Mahimabhaṭṭa's *Vyaktiviveka*
9. Rājaśekhara's *Kāvyamīmāṁsā*
10. Ānandavardhana's *Dhvanyāloka*
11. Abhinavagupta's *Abhinavabhāratī*
12. Viśvanātha's *Sāhityadarpaṇa*
13. Pt. Jagannātha's *Rasagaṅgādhara*

III. Philosophy

14. *Mīmāṁsāsūtra*
15. *Nyāyasūtra*
16. *Sāṅkhyasūtra*
17. *Vaiśeṣikasūtra*
18. *Yogasūtra*
19. *Vedāntasūtra*
20. Madhvācārya's *Sarvadarśanasaṁgraha*
21. *Tattvārthasūtra*
22. Dharmakīrti's *Pramāṇavārttika*
23. Jagadīśa's *Śabdaśakti-prakāśikā*

Dr. Rajnish Kumar Mishra's exposition of *Buddhist Theory of Meaning* was the **first Śāstra Group** research belonging to the 3rd part of the Objectives to be published in the ŚĀSTRA GROUP SERIES. Based on wide-ranging primary sources, including the Buddhist philosophical-epistemological texts in Sanskrit, the book sheds altogether new light on the Buddhist theory of meaning and, simultaneously argues against the fallacies that have cropped up around its latter-day interpretations. This book has great contemporary relevance for the post-structuralist debates.

Sadhna Parashar's translation of Rājaśekhara's *Kāvyamīmāṁsā* was published as the second Śāstra Group Publication. *Kāvyamīmāṁsā* is a seminal ninth-century text of literary theory; and it is different from the preceding texts in that for the first time, various issues and dimensions of literary creativity and composition are taken up for close analysis. The discussion is of great contemporary interest and is pertinent to issues of contemporary literary theory as well. This is the only complete translation of this important text and has for years been used by succeeding batches of students in the Centre of Linguistics and English. This book will, hopefully, lead to a renewal of Rājaśekhara studies and a revival of interest in related issues.

And the third book, Patañjali's *Yoga-sūtras,* published in the Śāstra Group Series was edited and translated by Dr. Saugata Bhaduri. *Yoga-sūtras* is basically, not about physical disciplining of the body, as has been popularly construed. It is a text of cognitive psychology, dealing with questions of knowledge — its nature, formation and validation. It is a short text but difficult to translate. Saugata Bhaduri has done a brilliant translation, noteworthy for its exactness and thoroughness.

I am very happy that now the fourth volume is being published in the Śāstra Group Series and it is a matter of great pride and satisfaction for me. Shri Debasish Chakrabarty has edited and translated Kaṇāda's *Vaiśeṣika-sūtra* with the required care and meticulousness. *Vaiśeṣika-sūtra* sets up an ontological system: its companion philosophy. *Nyāya* is an epistemological system. It enumerates and analyses 20 *dravya*, 5 *guṇa*, 5 *karma* and 7 attributes/ dimensions of *dravya, guṇa* and *karma.*

For an understanding of Indian ontological thinking, one has to study Vaiśeṣika, Sāṅkhya and Vedānta in conjunction with each other.

Vaiśeṣika is a materialist system but differs from Western meterialist systems in its being framed, like other Indian systems, by the *puruṣārtha* framework of the four ends of life — *dharma, artha, kāma,* and *mokṣa.* In fact, the very first *sūtra* says that the goal is to explain and expound *dharma.* In this sense Indian materialism is transcendental materialism.

Prof. Kapil Kapoor
Professor of English and Rector
Jawaharlal Nehru University
New Delhi - 110 067

Prefatory Essay

Six Indian Philosophical Systems and Kaṇāda's *Vaiśeṣika-sūtra*

Indian Philosophical Systems

THE word used for **philosophy** is *darśana* from the Sanskrit root *dṛś* which means 'to see' — **philosophy** means 'love of argument' and suggests an effort to impose a framework on the visible world/reality in order to make sense of it. *Darśana*, on the other hand, accords no constructive role to man's mind and means 'observation of things the way they are', to see them for what they are. As such it is very much an empirical inquiry and, contrary to the popular perception, its concerns are very concrete and this-worldly.

Indian philosophical systems fall into three schools — the brāhmaṇa (also called, in the tradition, the grammarians), the Buddhists and the Jains. The different philosophical systems can also be classified as (i) *āstika* (orthodox), and (ii) *nāstika* (heterodox). The parameter of orthodoxy, however, is different — acceptance of *śrutis* (Vedas) as *pramāṇa* (valid epistemology) is the criterion. Thus the Cārvāka, the Buddhist and the Jain systems are considered heterodox on this count. Three of the six orthodox schools — Mīmāṁsā, Vedānta, Sāṅkhya, Yoga, Vaiśeṣika, Nyāya — Mīmāṁsā, Sāṅkhya and Vaiśeṣika are *nirīśvara* (godless) schools, that is they do not posit 'god' as an ontological category and yet they are *āstika* because they accept Vedas as valid epistemology.

For each philosophical system, there is an authoritative text bearing the same name as the philosophical system itself and associated with a celebrated thinker as the author — Jaimini's

Mīmāṁsa-sūtra, Bādarāyaṇa's *Vedānta-sūtra*, Kapila's *Sāṅkhya-sūtra*, Patañjali's *Yoga-sūtra*, Kaṇāda's *Vaiśeṣika-sūtra*, Gautama's *Nyāya-sūtra*. We do not know when these texts were composed but it is safe to assume that they were composed in that age of empire building from 1000 BC onwards which was a period of great vigor and intellectual ferment and saw the formation of both political empires and intellectual systems. It is in this period that Pāṇini's *Aṣṭādhyāyī* was composed and in this age Buddha propounded his philosophy of useful action and good reason. These philosophical systems are the reasoned answers to some basic questions related to this **human** life in this world, questions that has been examined in a long tradition of philosophical inquiry that had its origins in the Upaniṣads.

Every system has a *sūtra* (text consisting of aphoristic statements), a *bhāṣya* (commentary) and a *vārttika* (elucidation of the commentary). A *sūtra* text states its truths in an extremely terse form so that the small text can be held in the mind. For this reason, it needs to be elucidated. The commentaries apart from explaining the text with examples often extend and enrich the original text and are studied as extensions of the original text. Thus, for example, the *Pūrva-Mīmāṁsā-sūtra* is by Jaimini, its *Bhāṣya* by Śabarasvāmin and its *Vārttika* by Kumārilabhaṭṭa.

Purpose and Nature of Philosophical Inquiry: Overcoming Suffering

It has been said, and it is widely believed, that the concerns of Indian philosophy are purely metaphysical and that their ultimate goal is to facilitate the achievement of *mokṣa* which is often translated as 'salvation'. Now the agenda of Indian systems, both theistic and atheistic, is the same — to find an answer to the problem of suffering of this, and in this, worldly life. The inquiry concerns this life and if some systems propound some metaphysical ontological categories like 'self' (*ātman*), 'the great self' (*paramātman*), etc., they argue that these are **real** instruments of alleviation of worldly suffering.

So the basic question that is addressed is the question of *duḥkha*, suffering. As is declared by the *Sāṅkhya-sūtra*,[1] the goal of human life (*puruṣārtha*) is to seek liberation (*nivṛtti*) from the three kinds of suffering — accidental, bodily, spiritual. We can do nothing about accidental suffering — an earthquake, for example. For bodily suffering, ailments of the body, the *Caraka-saṁhitā*, a text of *Āyurveda*, says we need *cikitsā*, medicinal treatment and for spiritual/mental suffering we need to study *darśana*, philosophy.

So the philosophical systems are each a different answer to this question of mental/spiritual suffering. All systems argue that **right knowledge** is the supreme means of liberation — they differ on the nature of this 'right knowledge'. But they all agree that this has to be a cognition of some ontological and epistemological truths by an individual knowing self. It is this awareness of what it is that immunes man to suffering, that makes him immune to those **causes** that make a man suffer. Suffering is inevitable — all that one can seek is the wisdom to rationalise suffering and reduce its potential to damage the self.

The Different Systems — Ontology and Epistemology

The word *veda* is from the verb-root *vid* which means 'to see'/'to know'.[2] *Veda* therefore means 'knowledge' and it is assumed to be non-contingent knowledge, that is knowledge free of time, place, individual. Vedic literature is classified into three broad divisions — *Mantra*s, *Brāhmaṇa*s and *Upaniṣad*s.

The knowledge embodied in these texts has been systematised and analysed by various thinkers and presented in the primary philosophical texts enumerated above. *Darśana*, philosophy, is defined as — *dṛśyate anena iti darśanam*, that is 'with the help of

1. *Sāṅkhya-sūtra*, 1.1.ff.
2. The same proto-Indo-European root *vid* underlies the English words 'visual'/'visualise'. The word 'seer' is an exact analogue of the Sanskrit word *draṣṭā* both with the meaning 'a wise man who apprehends knowledge directly'.

which the essential self (*tāttvika svarūpa*) of something is seen'. What is the starting point of Indian philosophy? Its meta-assumption is that all living beings tend towards *duḥkha-nivṛtti* (freedom from suffering).

So philosophy addresses the question of *duḥkha* (suffering). It concerns itself with four related issues:

(i) *heya* — the real nature of *duḥkha* (suffering).

(ii) *heyahetu* — the real cause of suffering.

(iii) *hāna* — what is the complete absence of suffering; what is that condition?

(iv) *hānopāya* — what is the means/method of achieving the complete absence of suffering.

In the examination of these questions, three ontological entities present themselves:

(i) *Cetana-tattva* — the life principle variously called *ātmā, puruṣa* (*jīva*). The question — who suffers? What is the nature of the one who suffers? Is suffering its natural property? The argument is that once one is face to face with this real self, one is in the state of complete absence of suffering, *hāna*.

(ii) *Jaḍa-tattva* — inert matter, *prakṛti*. That in which suffering originates, of which suffering is the necessary attribute. Not being able to distinguish between this inert matter and the life principle is the cause of suffering, *heyahetu*. Discriminating knowledge that enables a distinction between this and the life principle is the means of putting an end of suffering, *hānopāya*.

(iii) *Cetanā-tattva* — the great Self, variously called *paramātmā, īśvara, Brahman*. That which is the goal of the individual self, becoming one with which the individual self becomes autonomous of the inert matter and therefore immune to suffering.

In order to explain these four substantial concepts, the Śāstras, philosophical texts, explain the three *tattva*s, ontological entities, in precise, logical statements. Six of these philosophical systems are: Mīmāṁsā, Vedānta, Nyāya, Vaiśeṣika, Sāṅkhya, Yoga. These six are considered auxiliary to the study of Vedas. They are customarily classed into three sets of two related systems — Mīmāṁsā and Vedānta (Pūrva-Mīmāṁsā and Uttara-Mīmāṁsā); Vaiśeṣika and Nyāya; Sāṅkhya and Yoga.

Mīmāṁsā and Vedānta

Vedas teach three ways of living one's life: *karma-kāṇḍa* (the path of enjoined action); *upāsanā-kāṇḍa* (the path of devotion); *jñāna-kāṇḍa* (the path of knowledge).

Mīmāṁsā, known as Pūrva-Mīmāṁsā is the largest text — it has 2644 *sūtras* and 909 topics (*adhikaraṇa*). Its number of *sūtra*s is equal to those of the other five put together. In its 12 chapters it analyses *dharma*, which is announced as its subject by the very first *sūtra* — *athāto dharmajijñāsā*, 'heretofore, we investigate what is *dharma*'. According to Mīmāṁsā, *dharma* consists in the performance of enjoined actions by doing which one is able to sever the relation of self (*ātmā*)[*] with the body, the senses and the objects of senses. Therefore, Mīmāṁsā teaches *karma-kāṇḍa*, the manifold path of action; it teaches —

(i) *nitya-karma*, acts that should be performed everyday.

(ii) *naimittika-karma*, acts to be performed when some event takes place, like the birth of a child.

(iii) *kāmya-karma*, acts performed with some worldly or other-worldly end in view.

There are two other kinds of acts:

(iv) *niṣiddha-karma*, proscribed actions, acts proscribed by the Śāstras, and

(v) *prāyaścitta-karma*, acts performed to cleans one's self of the impressions (*saṁskāras*) left on the self by an indulgence in proscribed actions.

Maharṣi Jaimini says performance of the enjoined acts with faith would lead to 'heaven', bliss, here and now. Mīmāṁsā asserts that all knowledge is self-validated, for knowledge takes form only when necessary and sufficient conditions are present. Mīmāṁsā epistemology allows perception, inference, verbal authority (*śabda pramāṇa*), implication (*arthāpatti*). The Prābhākara School accepts analogy (*upamāna*) as the fifth epistemology. The (Kumārila) Bhāṭṭa School accepts in addition non-presence (*anupalabdhi*) as the sixth epistemology.

Mīmāṁsā accepts the externally existing world as real, accepts the material reality but does not accept a god (*paramātmā* or *īśvara*) as the creator of this universe which, Mīmāṁsā says, has always existed and therefore this universe (*jagat*) has had no beginning (*anādi*) and no end (*ananta*). Action is an independent power and it makes the world go.

Vedānta, also known as Uttara-Mīmāṁsā, is expressed in the Sūtras known varioulsy as *Brahma-sūtra, Śārīrika-sūtra, Vedānta-sūtra* attributed to Vyāsa known in the tradition as Bādarāyaṇa. Uttara-Mīmāṁsā teaches the path of knowledge, the knowledge of *Brahman* as its very first *sūtra* declares — *athāto brahmanjijñāsā*, 'heretofore we investigate what is *brahman*'. The topics treated are — *īśvara* (god), *prakṛti* (matter), *jīvātmā* (individual life principle), *punarjanma* (re-birth), states after death, *karma* (action), *upāsanā* (devotion/worship), *jñāna* (knowledge), *bandha* (bondage), *mokṣa* (liberation). Vedānta says suffering is the property of the material body (*jaḍa-tattva*), ignorance in the form of imposition of the body on the self (*ātmā*) is its cause, delinking one's self completely from the material body and establishing oneself in one's self constitutes the state of total absence of suffering, and to achieve this establishment in one's self, one must gain knowledge of the Great/Universal Self/Life Principle (*paramātma-tattva*) which is totally alien to the principle of sorrow.

The grand opposition of *dvaita~advaita* (dualism~non-dualism) concerns the relationship between the Individual Self and the Universal Self — in the state of *hāna* (complete absence of suffering), the two are argued to remain separate (dualism) or become one (non-dualism).

The central concept of Vedānta is *Brahman*. Sāṅkhya had posited two ultimate ontological categories — *prakṛti* (matter) and *puruṣa* (energy). Vedānta captures with great insight the fact that energy is not separate from but is in fact immanent in matter. *Brahman* is this one principle which subsumes both energy and matter. As such it is described in *Vedānta-sūtra*s as the substratum, the cause and the pervasive principle of the entire universe. This construct establishes the oneness of all being — the multiplicity (*nānātva*) and difference exist at the level of appearance. The source of this construct is to be found in the *Ṛgveda*, *puruṣasūkta* which conceives of a *puruṣa* which permeates the entire *brahmāṇḍa* (universe) and even beyond and all the inert and living entities are seen as parts or forms of that.

The first four *sūtra*s called *catuḥsūtrī* (1.1.1-4) generally state the substance of this concept of *Brahman*; the rest of the text is an explication. It is said —

> Now we will investigate *Brahman* (1.1.1); that which is the efficient cause (*nimitta*) of the origin, maintenance and destruction of this universe is *Brahman* (1.1.2); *Brahman* is established/proved by sister (1.1.3); the purpose of *śruti*s is establishment of *Brahman* (1.1.4).

This *Brahman* is described in its two aspects — in (a) its formless, attributeless (*nirguṇa*) aspect, and (b) its manifest (*saguṇa*) aspect. In its pure, attributeless, formless (*nirguṇa*) aspect, the non-manifest (*avyakta*) *Brahman* is beyond the dichotomy of form~formless (3.2.23).

Vedānta originated in the Upaniṣads but has continuously been commented upon and developed. Later a number of thinkers wrote their commentaries upon Jaimini's *sūtra*s and extended this system of thought. The greatest of them all, of course, is Ādi Śaṅkara who in his celebrated *Śārīrika-bhāṣya* established his non-dualist (*advaita*) principle:

(i) The multiplicity of the visible world is only a reflex of the one attributeless essence (*tattva*).

(ii) Inherent in the *Brahman* is its creative power (*māyā*) by which it appears in various manifest forms as so many cbjects.

(iii) So *Brahman* with its creative power (*māyā*) is the efficient cause of this universe.

(iv) The individual due to ignorance (*avidyā*), confuses his real self with his material body.

(v) On gaining knowledge of the oneness of *Brahman* and *ātmā* (*brahmātmaikatva*), the self-ness in the material body is lost leading to the extinction of *kartā-bhoktā* (doer-experiencer) awareness which in its turn frees man from the effect of his actions ending in his liberation from suffering.

The eleventh-century savant, Śrī Rāmānujācārya, the next great Vedānta-exegete modified the Śaṅkara principle by arguing the reality of the visible, material world. His principle has come to be known as Viśiṣṭādvaita. The third great original Vedānta-exegete is Śrī Madhvācārya who argued that the Universal Self (*Brahman*) and the Individual Self (*jīva*) are two different entities and consistently remain so. And as with Śrī Rāmānujācārya, the Madhvācārya principle accords primacy to *saguṇa* (manifest) divinity (*īśvara*) and therefore his followers are believers in ritual worship.

Vedānta, particularly Śaṅkara's *Advaita Vedānta* has had a very wide and deep influence on Indian life.

Sāṅkhya and Yoga

These two, says the *Bhagavad Gītā*, are the two most ancient systems and standing respectively for the paths of knowledge and of action. The first *sūtra* of Sāṅkhya says that as the proper knowledge of *tattva*s (the ontological entities) is the means of liberation from suffering, we will investigate what these *tattva*s are. As against the principle of intelligence that desires freedom from suffering, there is/must be the principle of matter, *prakṛti*, and the second and the third *sūtra*s described the eight-fold *prakṛti* and the sixteen *vikāra*s. Inert matter has two aspects — *prakṛti* (unmodified) and *vikṛti* (modified). That from which some other element is born is *prakṛti* and that finally formed element from which no other element can be born is *vikṛti*. After noting the 24 unmodified and the modified ontological elements, the fourth *sūtra* enunciates *puruṣa* as the twenty-fifth element, the 'intelligence'/'life' principle. The fifth *sūtra* (*traiguṇyam*) enunciates the all important doctrine of three-fold *prakṛti*, that three innate propensities (determining properties) belong to all the 24 elements.

The three *guṇa*s are *sattva, rajas, tamas* and in each ontological substance, modified and unmodified, one of these three properties predominates and the predominating property determines the nature and state of that substance. These *guṇa*s are dynamic principles and continually bring about change and produce result in and from the substances — they bring about the creation (*sṛṣṭi*) and destruction (*pralaya*). These three 'qualities' are accepted by all systems. *Sattva* denotes a state of perfection, of goodness, clarity, and serenity; *rajas* is all action, movement and passion; *tamas* is inertia, sloth and darkness. Sāṅkhya believes that in all beings a balance obtains among these three 'forces' and when an imbalance develops, undesirable consequences follow. This balance obtains in individuals, in 'systems', social, political, etc., and in the cosmos. This balance is the *ṛta* of the *Ṛgveda*. When this is disturbed, changes follow, desirable and undesirable, new elements may be formed, new conditions and factors come into play and there is great, restless flux till a new balance is achieved, that is the three inherent forces acquire a new equipoise. But Sāṅkhya does not tell us how this is to be achieved — through worship of *īśvara*, inquiry into one's self or through performance of enjoined actions. It does not go beyond telling us to be aware of the difference between the 'alert intelligence' (*puruṣa*) and 'inert matter' (*prakṛti*).

Yoga

It is Patañjali's Yoga system that informs us of the practical means of dissociating the Self, the alert intelligence or life principle from the inert matter, of the *sādhanā* to be followed to become aware of the difference. The concept of *īśvara*, absent in Sāṅkhya, is central in Yoga and devotion is an important construct in the method of bringing the mind under control.

There is much in common between Sāṅkhya and Yoga which accepts the 25 ontological elements. According to Sāṅkhya, a discriminating intellect is the instrument of liberation and this discriminating intellect is acquired only through the practice of *yoga*. What is *yoga*? *Yoga* is control of the tendency of the experiencing self to attach itself to the external objects so that the experiencing self (*citta*) becomes stabilised in its basic/native condition.

Yoga-sūtra has 159 *sūtra*s in four chapters. The first chapter, *Samādhipāda*, describes the nature of *yoga* and this is explained in the three *sūtra*s 2-4, the rest of the chapter being an explication of these three statements. '*Yoga* is control of the activity of the experiencing self' (1.1.2); 'In that state of control the experiencer is established in his native self' (1.1.3); 'Else, the experiencer becomes one with the activity of the self' (1.1.4). Stability of the mind or the self, its one-pointedness or focusing on **one** something (*ekāgratā*) is the great secret. *Ekāgratā* is keeping the mind engrossed in one thought to the exclusion of every other thought. The mind can focus on —

1. gross object,
2. subtle object/thought,

3. one's conscious self,
4. the inner self.

Unless the mind is so stabilised, the self will remain disturbed (*vikṣipta*) like the image of moon in turbulent water.

In the second chapter, *Sādhanapāda*, the method of regaining peace is laid down for those with *vikṣipta* (disturbed) self. Five causes of all suffering are enumerated —

1. ignorance (*avidyā*),
2. non-distinction between the material body and the self (*asmitā*),
3. desire for joys of the material body (*rāga*),
4. sorrows springing from non-fulfilment of material joys (*dveṣa*),
5. desire to protect the body for suffering (*abhiniveśa*).

Possible suffering should be renounced. The conjunction of the seer (*dṛṣṭā*) and what is there to see (*dṛśya*) is the cause of suffering. (2.16, 17) What is there to see? All this visible world (the 24 elements of Sāṅkhya) which is characterised by three-fold properties. The seer (*dṛṣṭā*) though intrinsically pure in its native self is permeated by the activities (*vṛtti*s) of the experiencing self. The indiscriminate coming together of the seer and the seen is due to lack of true knowledge or understanding. When one overcomes ignorance, one overcomes indiscriminate conjunction and that produces the absence of suffering. One overcomes ignorance by the highest form of discriminating intellect (*viveka-khyāti*). What is this high state of the Intellect (*prajñā*)? In this state —

1. All that was there to know has been known.
2. Whatever was to be distanced has been distanced.
3. Whatever was to be witnessed has been witnessed.

4. Whatever had to be done has been done; nothing more remains to be done.

5. The experiencing self has earned its right to liberation and no more right is there to be earned.

6. The properties of the experiencing self after fulfilling indulgence and liberation are beginning to dissolve back into their causes.

7. Free from the *guṇas*, the experiencing self is preparing to assimilate itself with the great Self.

In *sūtras* 29 to 55 of the second chapter, the five steps that constitute the outer phase of *yoga* are laid out. *Yama* is 'abstaining from violence, stealing, covetousness and telling truth and continence' (2.29). *Niyama* is 'purity, austerity, contentment, repetition of sacred words, devotion to God' (2.32). *Āsana* implies steadiness and comfort (2.46). Control of breath, of exhalation and inhalation is *prāṇāyāma* (2.49). *Pratyāhāra* is 'the restoration of sense to the original purity of mind by renouncing its objects' (2.54).

The third chapter, *Vibhūtipāda*, describes the other three steps, *dhāraṇā*, *dhyāna* and *samādhi*, together called *saṁyama*. 'Attention fixed upon an object is *dhāraṇā*' (3.1). 'Union of mind and object is *dhyāna*' (3.2). '*Samādhi* is that condition of illumination where union as union disappears, only the experience of the object on which the attention is fixed being present' (3.3). In *dhāraṇā*, the attention upon an object is disturbed; in *dhyāna*, the attention is not disturbed, but the consciousness of the thinker, the thinking and the object of thought are present; in *samādhi*, separate consciousness of the thinker, the thinking, the separate object disappear only the object, transformed by and transparent to thought, remains. By practising these, one acquires many powers (*siddhis*), but a true practitioner does not use them for these hinder his progress towards final illumination. 'These powers of knowledge are obstacles to illumination [enlightenment]; but illumination apart, they bring success' (3.37). 'Finally, by renouncing even these powers, the seed of bondage being destroyed, the *yogī* attains liberation' (3.50).

The final chapter, *Kaivalyapāda*, deals with the state of enlightenment/liberation. The self is freed of the agenthood, the role of the experiencer, of the participant becoming a pure observer. 'He who sees clearly, refuses to identify the mind with the self' (4.25). The individual then is also freed of self-consciousness — who am I/ what am I/how am I? Freed of this nothing remains to be achieved and — in the last of the nine states of consciousness described in the *Yoga-sūtras* — the *guṇa*s (the three qualities of being) dissolve in their own substratum/cause and this is liberation, the full revelation of the power of the self, its being only itself (*kaivalya*) (4.34). 'Mind without impurity and impediment, attains infinite knowledge; what is worth knowing in this world becomes negligible' (4.31).

Nyāya and Vaiśeṣika

These two systems have much in common. The Vaiśeṣika system concerns itself with ontology and Nyāya, accepting Vaiśeṣika ontology concerns itself with epistemological issues. The number of *Vaiśeṣika-sūtras* is 370 divided into ten chapters with two *āhnika*s (sections) in each chapter. The first part of the first chapter describes the properties and divisions of substances (*dravya*), qualities (*guṇa*) and actions (*karma*). In the second part of the first chapter, the general or universal is defined. Nine substances have been described in the second and third chapters, the atom theory (*paramāṇu-vāda*) in the first part of the fourth chapter, the transient substances in the second part of the fourth chapter, acts/actions in the fifth chapter, epistemological status of the Vedas and the constructs of *dharma-adharma* in the sixth, some qualities in the seventh and the eighth chapters, absence (*abhāva*) and knowledge (*jñāna*) in the ninth chapter and *sukha-duḥkha* (joy-sorrow) difference and their causes in the tenth chapter.

The word *vaiśeṣika* means indicator of different *padārtha*s (objects). *Padārtha*s are those that one cognises by perception.

Possession of the right knowledge of the six elements — substance, quality, action, universal, particular, and inseparable connection — will enable us to handle the problem of suffering. Vaiśeṣika is obviously a materialist system which posits atoms as the ultimate constituents of all objects.

Vaiśeṣika divides the object of knowledge (*prameya*), into seven *padārthas*: *dravya* (substance), *guṇa* (quality), *karma* (action), *sāmānya* (association), *viśeṣa* (difference), *samavāya* (inherence) and *abhāva* (non-existence).

1. *dravya* — earth, water, fire, space, time, direction, self and mind are the nine substances.
2. *guṇa* — colour, taste, smell, touch, number, measure, separateness, conjunction, division, distant, non-distant, gravitation, fluidity, oiliness/lubricity, sound, intellect, joy, sorrow, desire, enmity/repugnance, effort, *dharma* (righteousness), *adharma* (unrighteousness), *saṁskāra* (endowed power such as speed in air, etc., state of mind, restorative power as for example a branch of a tree which is held down goes back to its original position when release).
3. *karma* — five kinds of movement: upwards, downwards, constriction, expansion and change of place/going.
4. *sāmānya* — universal of a class of objects such as **treeness** of trees.
5. *viśeṣa* — specificity or particular.
6. *samavāya* — intimate union, and
7. *abhāva* — non-presence, absence.

Nyāya, it may be noted, also accepts these ontological categories. That is why these two systems go together — in these philosophical systems, truth consists in the nature of these *padārthas*; therefore, to get to know the truth, we must go to the root of these *padārthas*. To achieve this, we must make use of all valid *pramāṇas*, means of knowledge. *Padārthas* are divided into two — 'existent' and 'non-existent': the first six of the *padārthas* listed above belong to the 'existent' category while the seventh, *abhāva*, constitutes the 'non-existent' category. Of these seven, *dravya, guṇa* and *karma* belong to the category of *sat* or 'being'; that is, we can demonstrate their existence (qualities like 'happiness' and 'redness' can be shown to be existing in substances). Existence of the other four *padārthas* cannot be demonstrated.

Nyāya also says like Vaiśeṣika that truth will be known if we have knowledge of the *padārthas* and develop detachment that will lead to release, a state in which we know neither joy nor sorrow. Nyāya is also called Tarka-Śāstra — its main purpose being to establish by reasoning that the *kartā* or creator of all this world is Parameśvara. It is in this positing of *īśvara* that Nyāya differs from Vaiśeṣika. The Nyāya inquiry into truth is through the four *pramāṇas* or instruments of knowledge — *pratyakṣa* (perception), *anumāna* (inference), *upamāna* (analogy) and *śabda* (verbal testimony). But, predominantly, both Nyāya and Vaiśeṣika **conduct** inquiries through inference. Gautama Akṣapāda's *Nyāya-sūtra* has five chapters, with two sections in each chapter, in which the definition and characteristics of the following sixteen subjects are discussed:

> Objects of knowledge, means of knowledge, doubt, purpose, analogy, conclusion, part of a logical argument, argument, judgement, disputation (*vāda*), debate (*jalpa*), fallacious argument (*vitaṇḍa*), fallacious middle term (*hetvābhāsa*), deception, class, a fault in syllogism.

With proper knowledge of these sixteen objects, the self transcends hunger-thirst, greed-infatuation (*lobha-moha*), cold-heat and becomes liberated (*mukta*) and in that state joy-sorrow become non-existent. And this knowledge is attained by four means of knowledge — perception, inference, analogy and verbal testimony.

The basic principle of both Nyāya and Vaiśeṣika is *kārya-kāraṇa-vāda* (cause-effect theory) also called *paramāṇu-vāda* (atomist theory) which asserts that everything that exists has a prior cause. The ultimate cause or constituents of all gross material objects are subtle sub-atomic particles (*paramāṇu*). The conjunction of these particles in a hierarchic structure is accepted by these systems as the material cause of this visible universe. Of course, senses and *īśvara* are accepted as the two instrumental or efficient causes.

> Nyāya or Tarka (logic) gives rationalism its due place, but this does not lead to materialism, atheism or the Lokāyata system. Through intellectual inquiry, Nyāya comes to the conclusion that, if the world is so orderly with so many creatures in it, all of them interlinked, there must be an *īśvara* to have created it. Nyāya recognises that there are areas that cannot be comprehended by human reason and that the truths that cannot be established rationally must be accepted according to how Vedas see them. . . . Instead of idling away one's time without making any intellectual effort to discover the truth, would it not be better to keep thinking about things it be to arrive at the conclusion that there is no God? A person who does so is superior to the idler who has no intellectual concern whatsoever. Perhaps the atheist, were he to continue his inquiry, would develop sufficient intellectual clarity to give up his atheism. But the idler has no means of advancing inwardly.
>
> This is one reason why even 'Cārvākam' was accepted as a system. . . . Cārvākam believes that there is no need to worry about god or any spirit or to observe vows and fasts or to control one's senses. Live as you please according to your whims and according to the dictates of your senses.[3]

3. Pujyasri Chandrasekhara Sarasvati Svami, *Hindu Dharma. The Universal Way of Life*, Bombay: Bharartiya Vidya Bhavan, pp. 419-20.

The Answers to the Question — How to get rid of Suffering, here and now

Two questions are central to all philosophical inquiry — the nature and status of the universe, *jagat*, its materiality and its ultimate, 'total' reality, and secondly the relationship between man, his happiness, and this universe. As we noted at length in 1994,[4] each philosophical system asserts that a valid knowledge of this total reality is the most efficacious means of achieving *mokṣa*, liberation which in final terms amounts to freedom from suffering. Each system gives its own definition of this required knowledge. Mīmāṁsā asserts that it consists in the proper performance of enjoined acts of sacrifice and duty (*karma*). But right performance is possible only after a right knowledge of objects involved in the acts. Mīmāṁsā believes in the reality of the external world (*bāhya sattā*) — reality of the physical world is a fact of perception (*pratyakṣa*) and the objects of this world are either primordial or constructs of these primordial objects. In Vedānta (Uttara-Mīmāṁsā), this knowledge consists in the awareness that all the visible, diverse, multiple forms, objects both with and without life, are reflexes of the same **one** undifferentiated non-discrete Being (*sattā*) that permeates the entire universe. Sāṅkhya system describes the effort that leads to freedom from three kinds of *duḥkha* (sorrow), physical, spiritual and accidental. The effort must be directed at achieving a discriminating intellect (*viveka-jñāna*) which tells us that this entire visible creation is a product of *prakṛti* (matter) and *puruṣa* (spirit or life principle) interaction. *Prakṛti*, a modulation of 25 primordial elements, is characterised by three attributes (*guṇa*) which are in the original state but are modulated in interaction with the life-principle (*puruṣa*) so that one or the other attribute dominates and becomes the cause of suffering or happiness,

---

4. K. Kapoor, 'Concept of *padārtha* in Language and Philosophy' in *Sir William Jones Volume Commemorating the Bicentennary of His Death* (1794-1994). Bulletin of the Deccan College Post-Graduate & Research Institute, Pune, Vols. 54-5 (1994-5), pp. 197-221.

as the case may be. A proper **knowledge** of *puruṣa*, the essential self, enables one to see all suffering as unrelated to this essential self. But the discriminating intellect is not sufficient to free us of suffering — we need to meditate on the primordial elements, the objects of our discriminating intellect and strive to detach/dissociate our self from them. Yoga attributes our sorrows to the distractions of our *citta* and advocates, as the means of joy (*ānanda*), a disciplining of the *citta*'s potential to attach itself to objects of cognition. This disciplining depends on an understanding of the true nature of objects, on the ability to keep separate the *nāma* (designating world), *rūpa* (the form) and *jñāna* (knowledge/experience of the object). Progressively more evolved cognising consciousness, achieved through different forms of yogic meditation, enables one to achieve the discriminating intellect (*viveka-jñāna*) that frees us of the bondage of the word that filters indiscriminately into our self. Nyāya also seeks to liberate the self (*ātmā*) from the body, senses and the worldly object that constitute the objects of senses. The objects are either grasped by senses, in which case they are 'physically perceptible' or they are cognised by our mind, in which case they are 'mentally perceptible' but yet products of perception. This creation (*sṛṣṭi*) is a permutation of atoms (*paramāṇu*) and each object represents a particular permutation. Only a proper knowledge of the true nature of objects (*tattva-artha*) enables one to decide what is to be acquired or grasped and what is to be rejected and renounced. With the rise of such proper knowledge of the world, and of the self, one's self is no longer subordinate to one's consciousness and, therefore, does not experience either joy or sorrow, i.e., transcends the dichotomies and becomes one no longer subject to conflicts (*dvandvātīta*). The Vaiśeṣika system also seeks to show the path to cessation of sorrow through *tattva-jñāna*, a knowledge of the essential reality of the world. It divides all the worldly objects of knowledge into seven classes (and their sub-classes) and analyses the structure of these objects — their nature, properties and stages. The Jaina system says that *samyak-darśana*, proper and valid knowledge of the self, is the means of *mokṣa* which in the Jaina thought is the achievement of the natural pure self through a final cessation of *karma*, i.e., mental, verbal and bodily acts (see, *Tattvārtha-sūtra* 10.2). The Buddhists attribute all sorrows to 'ignorance' (*avidyā*) — the sorrows are 'real but it is possible to be unaffected by them by attaining or practising *nirvāṇa-mārga*, which includes proper or valid knowledge as the first stage of its eight-fold path. . . .

> Therefore in all the major Indian systems of thought . . . peace and happiness is attained only when we comprehend the true nature and totality of the objects that constitute the world around us and the substance of our cognitions.[5]

This Translation of *Vaiśeṣika-sūtra*

As part of the long-term project of making available in modern translations the important texts of the Indian intellectual traditions in English and other Indian languages to students and scholars of languages, literatures and cultures, this English translation of Kaṇāda's *Vaiśeṣika-sūtra* is being presented as the first venture. This is an important text because it is one text that deals with the theory of knowledge — and not in the abstract but in relation to human happiness. Knowledge has always been prestiged in the Indian tradition and has been accepted as the supreme means of salvation. This text is the only one that sets out a practical method, a set of practices to develop the necessary mental sufficiency to be able to 'know' something.

The Śāstra Group at JNU has a definite policy on these 'translations'. The goal is to communicate the intent and purport of the propositions as accurately and as clearly as possible so:

1. The technical terms have been retained in the main body of the text and these have been annotated comprehensively.

5. K. Kapoor, *op. cit.*, pp. 199-200.

This is the only way as one cannot expect equivalents to exist in a language of another intellectual tradition and, in any case such approximate one-word equivalents are bound to deviate the meaning.

2. The Sanskrit śāstric texts are composed in a most economical style and therefore eschew all the features of what is called these days 'textual binding', all the explicit and implicit connections that hold between adjacent and even separated statements. These features as the traditional scholars show in their commentaries are reconstructable from the context, from an understanding of the whole text and from a knowledge of the wider context of the subject of discussion. These 'understood' interconnections are a major obstacle for a lay student/reader of today. We have made them explicit and these have been formally shown as such through devices of punctuation. This makes reading easier.

3. Care has been taken to keep the language brief, precise and simple. As far as possible, the order of statement, including the order of *pada*s (morphological constructions/words) has been paralleled to the extent that is permissible in the different language, English.

Our next step would be to bring out these texts in two different ways —

(i) prepare script variants — that is, publish the original text in different Indian scripts, and

(ii) prepare 'translations' in major Indian languages.

Debasish Chakrabarty, the translator of this text, represents in this excellent, painstaking, exact, carefully considered translation the best of a young group of intellectuals perfectly at home in both the Western and the Indian traditions. I record here my deep appreciation of the quality of his mind and of his meticulous work.

Introduction to Vaiśeṣika-Sūtra

General overview

PHILOSOPHICAL enquiry, in India, began in the days of the earliest Upaniṣads. The Upaniṣads mark the epistemic shift from the Vedas and the *Brāhmaṇa*s in their focus on the notion of liberation of the soul.[1] The shift from the ritualistic to the more metaphysical form of enquiry found its takers in the various schools of philosophy that flourished around this period. The Upaniṣadic form of knowledge shifted its focus from the acceptance of the Vedas as revealed and controlled by rituals to knowledge as derivable from intuition, observation and analysis. The Upaniṣads were explorations in the search for enlightenment of the human condition and release from its bonds. Moving away from the *mantra* (verse) tradition, the Upaniṣads adopted the dialogue as their new form. The Upaniṣadic doctrines were concerned with the conceptualization of the other worlds, explorations of which would systematize the knowledge of the mundane world. It is in this milieu that the two classes of Indian philosophy, the theistic and the atheistic, came into being. While the atheists, namely the Buddhists, Jainas and Cāravākas (materialists), sought to establish their own authority, the theists,[2] considered the Vedas as their infallible authority.

The earliest texts of these theistic philosophies were essentially cogent, classified and arranged records of the viewpoints of a particular system collated from oral discussions and speculations of the progenitors of these systems, assembled by them or their disciples. The texts were probably intended for people who were well versed in the oral tradition and thus could easily follow the import of the suggestive phrases, aphorisms and allusions to the view of rival schools and their refutations. According to Surendranath Dasgupta:

> The fact that each system had to contend with other rival systems in order to hold its own has left its permanent mark upon all the philosophic literatures of India which are always written in the form of disputes. . . . At each step he [the author] supposes certain objections put forth against him, which he answers, and points out the defects of the objector or shows that the objection itself is ill founded. . . . Most often the objections of the rival schools are referred to in so brief a manner that those only who know the views can catch them.[3]

Kaṇāda's *Vaiśeṣika Sūtra*, our present concern, can be classified as a theistic text which does not believe in the existence of God and deals with physics and metaphysics. Tradition has it that major systems always look up to the basic text for the cardinal principles. The *Vaiśeṣika Sūtra* happens to be one such text that forms the basis of the syncretic Nyāya-Vaiśeṣika system that followed. To be accorded the status of a full-scale philosophical system, the concerns of the system ought to span a whole range: metaphysics, epistemology, ethics and theory of value, logic and philosophical method.[4] Though the *Vaiśeṣika Sūtra* provides the realist ontology, only when it is seen syncretically with the theistic, God-believing, Nyāya school (which provides the realist epistemology) can it be deemed a philosophical system. A philosophical system is also expected to develop its own metalanguage and reference mechanism whereby a tradition of commentary and expansion of its frontiers of knowledge are enabled. The syncretic Nyāya-Vaiśeṣika system deals with each of these areas extensively. In the *Vaiśeṣika Sūtra*, Kaṇāda develops a theory of atomicity, argues for a theory of sound and adapts an empiricist view of causality very much in the spirit of modern scientific enquiry.

A brief glimpse of the basic concepts of the *Vaiśeṣika Sūtra* would enable the reader to gauge for herself the parameters within which this philosophical system functions.

The *Vaiśeṣika Sūtra* compartmentalises knowledge into seven (6+1) categories: *dravya* (substance), *guṇa* (attribute), *karma* (action), *sāmānya* (generality), *viśeṣa* (particularity), *samavāya* (inherence) and the late addition, *abhāva* (non-existence).

A substance is the substratum of attributes and actions but is different from both. There are nine substances. Of these the first five, namely air, water, fire, earth, and ether are called the physical elements and all except ether, are composed of four kinds of atoms: air, water, fire, and earth. These atoms are indivisible and indestructible particles of matter and have the specific attributes of odour, taste, colour, touch and sound. The atoms are the indivisible part of a substance and are eternal and uncreated. According to Kaṇāda, atoms are too small to be perceived but must be inferred from their effects. He goes on to say that they may be without attributes, albeit temporarily. Later writers have likened atoms to extensionless mathematical points. Kaṇāda seems to have thought that the eternal nature of atoms depended upon their imperceptibility, since perceptible entities are destructible. Ether, direction, and time are imperceptible substances, which are eternal and all pervasive. The mind is an eternal substance but is as small as an atom — the internal sense directly or indirectly concerned with all physical functions of the body like cognition, feeling, etc. The self is an eternal and all-pervading substance, which is the substratum of the phenomenon of consciousness. The individual self is perceived internally by the mind of the individual. The world is created of atoms, the composition and decomposition of which explain the origin and destruction of the composed objects of the world. Atoms cannot move by themselves, the source of their motion being unseen forces, which operate according to the law of action.

Attribute is that which exists in a substance and has no attribute or action in itself. It can exist only in a substance. There is no action in attributes. Action, like attribute, belongs to substance and is of five kinds.[5]

A universal is the eternal essence common to all the individuals of a class. Particularity is the ground of ultimate differences of things. Ordinarily, we distinguish one thing from another by the peculiarities of its parts. Particularity stands for the individuality of the eternal entities of the world.

Inherence is a permanent or eternal relation by which a whole is in its parts, an attribute or an action is in a substance, the universal in the particulars and so on. The permanent relation between the universal and its individuals, and between attributes and actions and their substances is known as inherence. Finally, non-existence stands for all negative facts and is of four kinds.[6]

Whether the *Vaiśeṣika Sūtra* stands up to the scrutiny of 'a complete philosophical system', on its own, is debatable. Many scholars agree with Sarvepalli Radhakrishnan that,

> The defect of the Vaiśeṣika is that it does not piece together its results into a single coherently articulated structure. It is not a philosophy in the sense implied by the famous saying of the *Republic*

> that he who sees things together is the true dialectician or the philosopher. A catalogue of items is not a systematic philosophy. The many-sided context of human life is ignored by the Vaiśeṣika, and its physical philosophy and moral and religious values are not worked into a unified interpretation.[7]

However, other scholars hold that the syncretic Nyāya-Vaiśeṣika is 'a full-scale system' of Indian philosophy. Its contribution to all areas of philosophy is 'extensive' and is of 'fundamental importance'.[8] In fact, the Navya-Nyāya or the Neo-logical school, founded by Gaṅgeśa Upādhyāya (about AD 1225) with his famous treatise, *Tattvacintāmaṇi*, rose out of the ashes of the syncretic Nyāya-Vaiśeṣika school. About these later developments, Dr. Radhakrishnan says,

> The brief *sūtras* (of Gautama and Kaṇāda) set forth only the general and basic principles, epistemological and ontological, about things consistent with the viewpoint of the systems concerned. The other writers formulated their own views regarding the interpretation of the *sūtras* and other questions without violating their allegiance to the *sūtras*.[9]

As regards the metaphysics of the system, Potter is of the opinion that the 'Nyāya-Vaiśeṣika offers one of the most vigorous efforts at the construction of a substantialist, realist ontology that the world has ever seen'.[10] The Vaiśeṣika ontology admits repeatable properties and is realistic in nature, that is, it conceptualises the world as created from timeless entities, spatial points and temporal events. The epistemological debates on the idealist critique of the substance between the Nyāya-Vaiśeṣika schools and the Buddhists are perhaps one of the most important confrontations in the history of Indian Philosophy. The Nyāya-Vaiśeṣika system does not engage the disputations on ethical theory *per se* as it was not the primary focus of the system, yet the system does present arguments regarding issues such as belief in transmigration, *karma* and the possibilities of liberation. Though Vaiśeṣika argues in accordance with the tenets of the system of logic, the torchbearer of the theory of philosophical debate in the Indian tradition is the Nyāya system. In fact, the system grew as one that specifically studied the theory of argumentation. It needs to be understood here that there was a peculiar system of division of labour that the ancient Indian seers formulated. Accordingly, the domains of inquiry of one school did not always overlap with the concerns of the others. So while the Mīmāṁsakas dealt with ethical systems, logic and argumentation was the forte of the Naiyāyikas. The question of philosophical method has been of interest to philosophers (Western and Eastern) for ages. The 'linguistic turn' has been hailed as a unique phenomenon in the history of philosophy.[11] The concern with the theories of meaning, syntax, semantics and pragmatics has been a preoccupation with the Indian thinkers since long. Maybe that is the reason why the Vaiyākaraṇas (grammarians) are considered a philosophical school in themselves. The Nyāya system too looks critically at the empirical theories of validity and truth. The syncretic system opposes the uncritical use of intuition and appeals to revelation.

The Nyāya-Vaiśeṣika theory of the world, through its atomic theory attempts to explain only the composite objects of the world that are non-eternal. It certainly is one of the earliest theories in philosophy to look at the concept of atomicity, yet the Vaiśeṣika Sūtra certainly would not stand the scrutiny of the modern empirical understanding of atomic theory or atomic structure. Speaking pointedly about the atomic theory of the syncretic Nyāya-Vaiśeṣika system, Sarvepalli Radhakrishnan says,

> In its attempt to explain the origin and destruction

of the world, it reduces all composite objects to the four kinds of atoms of earth, water, fire and air. So it is called the atomic theory of the world. But it is not a mechanistic or materialistic theory like atomism of Western science and philosophy. It does not ignore the moral and spiritual principles governing the processes of composition and decomposition of atoms.[12]

Date of the Vaiśeṣika Sūtra

The date of such an ancient text cannot be fixed with any certainty, though scholars are perfectly certain that the *Vaiśeṣika Sūtra* was written before Caraka's *Sūtrasthāna* (AD 80). Scholars contend that the *Vaiśeṣika Sūtra* was written before the *Nyāya Sūtra*, which was known to Kauṭilya in some form of commentary in 300 BC. Certain scholars like Vidyābhūṣana think that Gautama (author of the *Nyāya Sūtra*) flourished at around 555 BC, which would then place Kaṇāda at around 600 BC. Some Chinese scholars like Chi-Tsan date the *Vaiśeṣika Sūtra* at about 800 years before Buddha. In any case, scholars think that there is ample evidence to prove that the *Vaiśeṣika Sūtra* is pre-Buddhist and can be dated approximately between 600 BC to 200 BC.

The Text and the Author

Vaiśeṣika, the name of the system, has been interpreted in two ways. One explanation is derived from the fifth category, *viśeṣa*, used in the sense of 'particularity'. Another view is that the name of the system is derived from the category *viśeṣa*, on which the conception of the atomic theory is based. In the latter case *viśeṣa* is interpreted as 'special'. Whatever be the point of view, *viśeṣa* as a category is diametrically opposed to the category of *sāmānya* (universal). *Viśeṣa* is that underived peculiarity that explains the differences of partless eternal substances like space, time, souls, minds and atoms of similar kind. Udayana, in *Kiraṇāvali,* is of the opinion that *viśeṣa* is as imperceptible as the atom.

The founder of this school, probably a fictitious person, is popularly known as Kaṇāda, the eater of *kaṇa*s. The word *kaṇa,* according to Śrīdhara, means grain. Kaṇāda supposedly lived on grains picked up from the roadside. Or more appropriately, the word *kaṇa* may mean atom; Kaṇāda would then be an atom-eater, and that as the nickname of the founder of the system, would suggest his association with the atomic theory. According to the tradition preserved in the Buddhist writings, the name of the founder of the Vaiśeṣika system was Ulūka, and the system has also been known as Aulukya. It has been speculated that the name, Ulūka or owl, was given to him because he worked during the day and scoured for his food at night. The Hindu philosophical tradition associates Kaṇāda with Benaras and Gautama or Akṣapāda ('eyes in his feet'), the author of the *Nyāya Sūtras,* with Mithila. Both these places were influential seats of learning and many of the later torchbearers of the system hailed from these two centres.

Structure of the text

The *Vaiśeṣika Sūtra* has 373 aphorisms divided into ten chapters. Each chapter has two lessons. The style of the *sūtra*s is quite laconic and many of the later Vaiśeṣika authors found it rather difficult to understand. The aphorisms are very dense and this perhaps has given the translators and commentators room to metaphysicize. Most aphorisms are linked to the previous one. In certain cases the author first establishes his view, then presents the objections and finally establishes the view by disproving the objections. All the categories and statements are established in the aphorisms and not merely stated.

Beginning with the purpose of explaining *dharma,*[13] the first chapter of the *Vaiśeṣika Sūtra* lays down the principal categories. Then it goes on to enumerate the three prime categories — substance, attribute and action, as well as their common properties and differences, and so on. In the second lesson, the reader is introduced to the concepts of cause and effect, generality and specificity, and being in substance, attribute and action.

The second chapter is a detailed discussion on the nature and mark of the nine substances — earth, water, fire, air, ether, time, direction, self and mind. The second lesson ends with a discussion on the non-eternality of sound. The third chapter is a detailed examination of the self and the mind.

The description of Nature, establishment of the existence and eternality of atoms, and the explanation of how sensory perception leads to knowledge make up the first lesson of the fourth chapter. The second lesson consists of the composition and types of bodies. The fifth chapter is on action and the next chapter deals with the concepts of giving, receiving, renunciation, and seen and unseen deeds that produce merit.

Attributes are enumerated in the seventh chapter. There is a detailed discussion in the first lesson on atomicity, the sizes of ether, mind, direction and time. Inherence as a substance is examined in the second lesson. The various types of cognition and negation are dealt with in the eighth and the ninth chapters respectively. The tenth chapter dwells upon the notions of pleasure and pain and a detailed study of cause. Kaṇāda's reasserting remarks on the authoritativeness of the Vedas mark the end of the *Vaiśeṣika Sūtra.*

Syncretism: the Vaiśeṣika and the Nyāya Philosophies

A. ALLIED SYSTEMS

saṁvid eva hi bhagavati vastūpagame naḥ śaraṇam

> Experience is the sole criterion of our acceptance of the reality of external objects.[14]

This is the basic guiding principle of the Nyāya-Vaiśeṣika materialism. We are presented a world that consists of individual objects called substances. These substances appear as the substrata of certain properties in relation of the container and the contained: they cannot be identical but must differ in essence. Essential difference between the substratum and its properties is the cornerstone of the structure of materialism. For instance, clay is the substratum while the pot is the manifestation of its properties. Substances are always the substrata but the properties residing in them are of various kinds. Some are stationary attributes, like colour, and some are transient in nature, like any action. Some objects in our common experience are so similar that they are designated by a common noun and have something in common to all individuals of that class, regarded as generality. The particular is a special property that differentiates one atom from another in spite of their being of the same class. Of these five categories, the last four, namely *guṇa, karma, sādhāraṇa* and *viśeṣa* (apart from substance), being properties, are found residing in the substrata of the substances. The relation between the substratum and the substance is one of connection — therefore a sixth category, inherence, was assumed. To these six categories later Nyāya-Vaiśeṣika theorists added a seventh, non-existence (*abhāva*).

The Vaiśeṣika School changes much of its character once in contact with the followers of the Nyāya School. The need to present a syncretic front arose perhaps due to the persistent attacks of the followers of the Mīmāṁsā and the Sāṅkhya schools. While Vaiśeṣika gained immeasurably from the logic, ethics and the theory of meaning of the Naiyāyikas, the Nyāya School used the categories of the realist ontology of Vaiśeṣika to build up their system.

'A system', according to Karl H. Potter, 'is a set of concepts which are interrelated so as to explain what needs to be explained fully, accurately and with no waste motion.'[15] The methodological choices which a philosopher must make, would, according to Potter, include the logic to be availed of and the elements to be dealt with. So far as logic is concerned, the later Naiyāyikas perfected a system in which every technical term had a referent. They did not see ontology as determined by a list of things named by nouns only, but also construed verbs as naming entities. They were not suspicious of repeatable entities such as universals either.

The Vaiśeṣika ontology, which provided the elements of this syncretic system, was guided by a simple dictum: basic elements must have no constituents. This dictum led the Vaiśeṣikas to view the ultimate component out of which material things are produced as atomic. They viewed time, space, self and internal organs as elements too. They also admitted relations and the objects of relations into the basis of the system.

The syncretic Nyāya-Vaiśeṣika system moved from strength to strength down the ages, more so after a regular string of debates began with the Buddhist tradition. These encounters resulted in a much-detailed evaluation of the system in the works of scholars like Vātsyāyana (AD 450-500), Candramati (AD 450-500), Uddyotakara (AD 550-610), Jayanta Bhaṭṭa (AD 840-900), and Udayana (AD 1050-1100), but the point of reference has always remained the works of the pioneers: Kaṇāda's *Vaiśeṣika Sūtra* and Gautama's *Nyāya Sūtra*.

The two schools, Nyāya and Vaiśeṣika, were separate in their origin as well as in their early course of development. While the Nyāya school was chiefly concerned with the method of debate and syllogism, the Vaiśeṣika school formulated its ontological structure on the basis of six categories which have been accepted as the basis of materialism by the syncretic Nyāya-Vaiśeṣika school. A close relation between the two schools seems to have existed from the earliest times, hence they have been always considered as allied systems.

B. DIFFERENCES

In spite of being allied systems there are certain basic differences that need to be highlighted. Whereas the *Vaiśeṣika Sūtra* is a much more homogeneous work, in the *Nyāya Sūtra* two or three different streams of purposes have met — for instance, the treatment of debate as a practical art, the various types of futility and the points of an opponent's refutation, the polemic against various doctrines, etc. While the *Nyāya Sūtra* advocates methods of Yoga, the Vaiśeṣika does not do so though it defines Yoga (5.2.16). While the former gives an extremely perceptive definition of perceptual knowledge, the latter considers it to be produced by the close proximity of the self, the senses and the objects of sensory perception. Inference is classified into three — inference of an unperceived effect from a perceived cause, inference of an unperceived cause from a perceived effect and inference based on non-causal uniformity (inference, as a category, remains undefined in the *Nyāya Sūtra*). The Vaiśeṣika on the other hand does not classify but gives only particular types or instances. While the *Vaiśeṣika Sūtra* does not consider sound as proof separately but admits the validity of the Vedas (which is itself a manifestation of sounds), the *Nyāya Sūtra* considers the proof of sound as not only applicable to the Vedas but also the testimony of any trustworthy person — the seers, the royalty, outsiders, etc. The Naiyāyikas propound other proofs too but the Vaiśeṣikas do not seem to know of them. *Nyāya Sūtra* claims that non-existence can be directly perceived. *Vaiśeṣika Sūtra* on the other hand holds that perception of non-existence is through the perception of the locus to which it refers. The Nyāya philosophy says nothing about the six categories, while the Vaiśeṣika philosophy is based on them. Nyāya proves the materiality of senses and attempts to prove the existence of God, while Vaiśeṣika merely touches upon the materiality of senses briefly and does not even mention God. The concept of atoms is dealt with explicitly in the *Vaiśeṣika Sūtra*, while Nyāya briefly touches upon the topic. Salvation is referred to as liberation in the *Nyāya Sūtra* and is the cessation of pain, while *Vaiśeṣika Sūtra* refers to it as the unsurpassed state — the permanent cessation of connection with the body.

Vaiśeṣika and Pūrva-Mīmāṁsā: Relations

The *Vaiśeṣika Sūtra* begins with the statement that its objective is to elaborate on *dharma*. This is also the express purpose of Jaimini in the *Mīmāṁsā Sūtra*. A comparative study of the first three aphorisms would be as follows:

athāto dharma jijñāsā ।

Now, then we will enquire into *dharma*.
— Jaimini

athāto dharma vyākhyāsyāmaḥ ।

Now, then, we will explain *dharma*.
— Kaṇāda

codanālatho artho dharmaḥ ।

That which is prescribed by the Vedas is *dharma*.
— Jaimini

yato'bhyudaya niḥśreyasa siddhiḥ sa dharmaḥ ।

That from which an elevation and an unsurpassed state is attained, is *dharma*. — Kaṇāda

tasya nimittaparīṣṭiḥ ।

Examination is the proof of that (*dharma*).
— Jaimini

tadvacanād āmnāyasya prāmāṇyam ।

Authoritativeness belongs to the Vedas because it is a declaration of that (*dharma*). — Kaṇāda

Many scholars refer to these striking similarities in the openings of the two texts as the basis for their argument that Vaiśeṣika may have been an old school of Mīmāṁsā. They say there is not the slightest trace of the structure of realist metaphysics as distinguished from epistemology in Mīmāṁsā. So, to challenge idealism, by the side of many sciences that were subsidiary to the science of sacrifice, there was formulated within the fold of Pūrva-Mīmāṁsā school, a system of realistic categories. For, the Pūrva-Mīmāṁsakas say that otherwise the disjunction between the first three aphorisms and the description of categories in the fourth aphorism is unexplainable. They say:

dharmam vyākhyātu kāmasya satpadārthopavarṇanam himavad gantukāmasya sāgara gamanopanam ।

For one who intends to expound *dharma*, the description of the six categories is like an attempt of one, who intending to go to the Himālayas, directs his step to the sea.[16]

Some of the main points in which Mīmāṁsā differs from the syncretic Nyāya-Vaiśeṣika system are — (a) self-validity of the Vedas; (b) eternality of the Vedas; (c) disbelief in any creator or God; (d) eternality of sound; (e) direct perception of the self in the notion of the ego. Of these the first and second points do not form any subject of discussion in the *Vaiśeṣika Sūtra*. As no God is mentioned and as the unseen is based on the authority of the Vedas, *Vaiśeṣika Sūtra* has no conflict with the *Mīmāṁsā Sūtra*. Vaiśeṣika has no conflict with the Mīmāṁsā in the third point too. As far as the direct perception of the self in the notion of the ego is concerned, the tradition of the Nyāya-Vaiśeṣika view is that the self is supposed to exist because it must be inferred as the seat of the attributes of pleasure and pain, etc. But the arguments given are that the existence of the self is first inferred by reason of its activity, and the existence of pleasure, pain, etc. (3.2.4). In 3.2.6-7 this is challenged, saying that no certainty can be arrived at since we cannot distinguish between the perception of this activity by the self or by the body. In 3.2.8 it is suggested that the existence of the soul should be accepted on the authority of the scriptures. And finally in 3.2.10-18 the *Vaiśeṣika Sūtra* concludes that our feeling as 'I' is proof of direct perception of the self and need not depend on the scriptures. But these arguments are, one thinks, a bit far-fetched — Kaṇāda's aphorisms are as such a cogent whole as he tries to explain *dharma* through our perception of daily and mundane realities. As regards the question of the eternality of sound, some scholars believe that Kaṇāda in 2.2.25-32 gives arguments in favour of non-eternality of sound but from 2.2.33-37 he closes in favour of eternity of sound. This is a clear misreading of the text based on faulty division of the sutras. If the aphorisms are read as they are presented in Madhvācārya's *Sarvadarśanasaṁgraha*, the arguments become quite clear. The two aphorisms responsible for this rampant misinterpretation are 2.2.36 and 37. Instead of being read as:

sandigdhaḥ — 2.2.36

sati bahutve saṅkhyābhāva sāmānyataḥ
— 2.2.37

They ought to be read as:

sandigdhaḥ sati bahutve — 2.2.36

saṅkhyābhāva sāmānyataḥ — 2.2.37

> All these arguments (for the eternal nature of sound) are doubtful. — 2.2.36
>
> (As sounds) commonly exist (as) enumerable. — 2.2.37

Thus the non-eternal nature of sound is re-established. Moreover this is exactly the style, which Kaṇāda follows (for example, also see 3.2.12-14, 3.2.15-17 and 7.2.4-6). In this light the sudden deviation above would clearly seem illogical.[17] So one can say that these arguments are rather stretched in order to accommodate the proposition that the Vaiśeṣika is an old school of the Mīmāṁsā.

Nyāya-Vaiśeṣika Literature

There are three periods in the Nyāya-Vaiśeṣika literature:

(a) The period of origin (600 BC — AD 610), in which were written the *Vaiśeṣika Sūtra* by Kaṇāda, *Nyāya Sūtra* by Gautama, Vātsāyana's *Bhāṣya* on *Nyāya Sūtra,* Prasastapāda's *Padārthadharmasaṁgrahạ,* Gaṅgādhara Kavirāja's *Bhāradvāja Vṛttī* and *Kiraṇāvali.*

(b) In the period of conflict with the Diññāga school (AD 650 — 1200), Kumārilabhaṭṭa wrote *Slokavārttika,* Prabhākara wrote *Bṛhatī.* Vācaspatimiśra's *Nyāyavārttikatātparyaṭīkā,* Upaskara's *Nyāyasūcinibandha,* Jayanta's *Nyāyamañjarī,* Bhāsarvajña's *Nyāyasāra,* Udayana's *Lakṣaṇāvalī, Nyāyakusumāñjalī, Nyāyapariśiṣṭa,*

Nyāyavārttikatātparyaṭīkāpariśuddhi, Śivāditya's *Lakṣaṇamālā* and Śrīdhara's *Nyāyakandalī* were written in this period.

(c) The post-Buddhist period (after AD 1300) saw Varadarāja's *Tārkikarakṣa,* Vallabhācārya's *Nyāyalīlāvatī*), Śaśadhara's *Nyāyasiddhāntadīpa* and Gaṅgeśa's *Tattvacintāmaṇi.* There was a decline in Nyāya-Vaiśeṣika literature in the eighteenth century. It was not until the nineteenth century that it recovered as a highly technical syllogistic philosophy.

Translator's Note

A few things have been kept in mind while translating the text. The effort has been to stay as close as possible to the spirit and the feel of the original *sūtra.* Wherever additional words had to be added for the benefit of syntax, they are placed in parentheses. Subtitles have been added to simplify the arguments by grouping the *sūtras* in cogent sections. Technical terms in most cases have been retained in their Sanskrit original and footnotes provided at the first occurrence of the word. In most cases the footnotes hint at semantic approximations and not absolutes. The translator accepts the sole responsibility for any fallacy in interpretation and translation of the text.

Finally . . .

Kaṇāda in *Vaiśeṣika Sūtra* keeps very close to material aspects and definitions. The text is written, keeping in mind the definition it coins for knowledge, as an effect like any other effect and its origin or production occurring in the same way as any other effect, namely, by a joint collocation of intellectual and physical causes. This text is the earliest exposition on physics in Indian philosophy. It has been said that just as Pāṇini's grammar is indispensable for a proper knowledge of linguistic science, similarly, Kaṇāda's

Vaiśeṣika Sūtra is indispensable for knowing the true nature of categories.

References

1. Romila Thapar, 'Sacrifice, Surplus and the Soul', in *History of Religions,* Vol. 33 No. 4, ed. Frank, E. Reynolds, Wendy Doniger, Gary L. Ebersole, Bruce Lincoln, Chicago, 1996.
2. There were six theist schools that were further subdivided into those who believed in God and those who did not. In the former category belonged the Yoga, Vedānta and the Nyāya schools, while the Sāṅkhya, Mīmāṁsā and the Vaiśeṣika schools belonged to the latter.
3. Surendranath Dasgupta, *A History of Indian Philosophy,* Vol. I, Delhi, 1922, p.66.
4. Karl. H. Potter, 'Introduction', *Encyclopedia of Indian Philosophies: Indian Metaphysics and Epistemology: The Tradition of Nyāya-Vaiśeṣika up to Gangeśa*, Delhi, 1997, p. 1.
5. Namely, rising, falling, contraction, expansion and movement (from one place to another).
6. Cf. 9.1.1-5. They are: *prāgbhāva, dhvaṁsābhāva, anyonyābhāva* and *atyantābhāva.*
7. Sarvepalli Radhakrishnan, *Indian Philosophy,* Vol. II, New York, 1977, pp. 246-47.
8. Karl. H. Potter, *op. cit.*, p. 1.
9. Sarvepalli Radhakrishnan, and board (eds.), *History of Philosophy Eastern and Western,* Vol. I, London, 1967, p. 231.
10. Karl. H. Potter, *op. cit.*, pp. 1-2.
11. *Ibid.*
12. Sarvepalli Radhakrishnan, 1967, p. 227.
13. Variously translated as nature of being, virtue, merit, and duty. In this translation we will retain the original Sanskrit term with the sole intention of keeping the sense intact.
14. Vācaspatimiśra, *Nyāyavārtikatātparyaṭīkā* 2.2.36, as quoted by Sriram Sharma in his 'Introduction' to *Vaiśeṣika Darśana*, Bareilly, 1990. Translation, mine.
15. Karl. H. Potter, *op. cit.*, p. 38.
16. Quoted in the introduction by Sriram Sharma to *Vaiśeṣika Darśana*, Bareilly, 1990, p. 11.
17. This methodology of presenting objections followed by the defence has been established earlier in this introduction (see the section *GENERAL OVERVIEW*).

प्रथम अध्याय – First Chapter

प्रथम आह्निक[1] – First Āhnika

[1] अथातो धर्मं व्याख्यास्यामः ॥ १ ॥

athāto dharmaṁ vyākhyāsyāmaḥ ॥1 ॥

Now we will explain *dharma*.[2]

[2] यतोऽभ्युदयनिःश्रेयससिद्धिः स धर्मः ॥ २ ॥

yato'bhyudayaniḥśreyasasiddhiḥ sa dharmaḥ ॥2 ॥

That is *dharma* (which leads to the) attainment of *abhyudaya*[3] and *niḥśreyasa*[4].

[3] तद्वचनादाम्नायस्य प्रामाण्यम् ॥ ३ ॥

tadvacanādāmnāyasya prāmāṇyam ॥3 ॥

That (teaching/tradition/collection) which explains this (*dharma*) is authoritative (*pramāṇa*).[5]

Enumeration of Padārthas[6]

[4] धर्मविशेषप्रसूताद् द्रव्यगुणकर्मसामान्यविशेषसमवायानां पदार्थानां साधर्म्य वैधर्म्याभ्यां तत्त्वज्ञानान्निःश्रेयसम् ॥ ४ ॥

---

1. Division.
2. *Dharma* has many meanings, law, practice, custom, duty, virtue, moral merit, etc. Here the nearest equivalent is righteous.
3. Be elevated, go up from one particular present state to another, a higher state well-being.
4. Final emancipation. Also cf. *mokṣa*.
5. Valid sources of knowledge.
6. Ontological categories.

dharmaviśeṣaprasūtād dravyaguṇakarmasāmānya-viśeṣasamavāyānāṁ padārthānāṁ sādharmya vaidharmyābhyāṁ tattvajñānān niḥśreyasam ॥4॥

The true knowledge of shared and differing properties of ontological categories, based in/generated by the particular attributes of those *padārthas* — *dravya,*[7] *guṇa,*[8] *karma,*[9] *sāmānya,*[10] *viśeṣa*[11] and *samavāya*[12] — is productive of *niḥśreyasa.*

Enumeration of the Dravyas, Guṇas, Karmas

[5] पृथिव्यापस्तेजो वायुराकाशं कालो दिगात्मा मन इति द्रव्याणि ॥ ५ ॥

pṛthivyāpastejo vāyurākāśaṁ kālo digātmā mana iti dravyāṇi ॥5॥

Pṛthvī,[13] *āpa,*[14] *teja,*[15] *vāyu,*[16] *ākāśa,*[17] *kāla,*[18] *dik,*[19] *ātmā,*[20] and *mana*[21] are the *dravyas.*

[6] रूपरसगन्धस्पर्शाः संख्यां परिमाणानि पृथक्त्वं संयोगविभागौ परत्त्वाऽपरंत्वे बुद्धयः सुखदुःखे इच्छाद्वेषौ प्रयत्नाश्च गुणाः ॥ ६ ॥

rūparasagandhasparśāḥ saṁkhyāṁ parimāṇāni pṛtha-

7. Substance.
8. Attribute.
9. Action.
10. General.
11. Particular.
12. Inherence.
13. Earth.
14. Water.
15. Energy, fire.
16. Air.
17. Ether, sky.
18. Temporal co-ordinates, time.
19. Spatial co-ordinates, direction.
20. Self.
21. Mind.

ktvaṁ saṁyogavibhāgau parattvā'paratve buddhayaḥ sukhaduḥkhe icchādveṣau prayatnāśca guṇāḥ ॥6 ॥

Form or colour, taste, odour, touch, number, measure, distinctiveness, conjunction, disjunction, *paratva,*[22] *aparatva,*[23] intellect, *sukha,*[24] *duḥkha,*[25] desire, aversion, effort, etc.,[26] are the *guṇa*s.

[7] उत्क्षेपणमवक्षेपणमाकुञ्चनं प्रसारणं गमनमिति कर्माणि ॥ ७ ॥

utkṣepaṇamavakṣepaṇamākuñcanaṁ prasāraṇaṁ gamanamiti karmaṇi ॥7 ॥

Movement upwards (rise), movement dowanwards (fall), contraction, expansion and movement (from one place to other) are the *karma*s.

[8] सदानित्यं द्रव्यवत् कार्यं कारणं सामान्यविशेषवदिति द्रव्यगुणकर्मणामविशेषः ॥८ ॥

sadānityaṁ dravyavat kāryaṁ kāraṇaṁ sāmānya-viśeṣavaditi dravyaguṇakarmaṇāmaviśeṣaḥ ॥8 ॥

Sat,[27] *anitya,*[28] substantive, effect, cause, *sāmānya,*[29] *viśeṣa,*[30] are peculiar to *dravya, guṇa* and *karma*.

---

22. Otherness.
23. Non-otherness.
24. Happiness, pleasure.
25. Unhappiness, sadness, pain.
26. The, *etc.*, here are considered by various commentators as referring to other common *guṇa*s (seven) implied in the use of *ca* — *gurutva* (heaviness), *dravatva* (fluidity), *sneha* (oiliness), *saṁskāra* (elasticity), *dharma* (*op. cit.*, 2n), *adharma* (demerit) and *śabda* (word, sound). Thus there are 24 *guṇa*s.
27. Existent.
28. Non-eternal, transitory.
29. Generality.
30. Particularity.

Properties of Dravya, Guṇa and Karma

[9] द्रव्यगुणयोः सजातीयारम्भकत्वं साधर्म्यम् ॥ ९ ॥

dravyaguṇayoḥ sajātīyārambhakatvaṁ sādharmyam ॥9 ॥

Dravya and *guṇa* generate substances of their own class (which is) a common property (shared by them).

[10] द्रव्याणि द्रव्यान्तरमारभन्ते गुणाश्च गुणान्तरम् ॥ १० ॥

dravyāṇi dravyāntaramārabhante guṇāśca guṇāntaram ॥10 ॥

Dravya generates *dravya* and *guṇa* too (generates) other *guṇas*.

[11] कर्म कर्मसाध्यं न विद्यते ॥ ११ ॥

karma karmasādhyaṁ na vidyate ॥11 ॥

Karma cannot be formed by *karma.*

[12] न द्रव्यं कार्यं कारणं च बधति ॥ १२ ॥

na dravyaṁ kārya kāraṇaṁ ca badhati ॥12 ॥

And neither is *dravya* destroyed by its effect or its cause.

[13] उभयथा गुणाः ॥ १३ ॥

ubhayathā guṇāḥ ॥13 ॥

(But) *guṇas* (are destroyed) by both (effect and cause).

[14] कार्यविरोधि कर्म ॥ १४ ॥

kāryavirodhi karma ॥14 ॥

Effect (*karma*'s) is opposed by *karma.*

[15] क्रियागुणवत् समवायिकारणमिति द्रव्यलक्षणम् ॥ १५ ॥

kriyāguṇavat samavāyikāraṇamiti dravyalakṣaṇam ॥15 ॥

(Having) actions, *guṇa*s and (being) coinherent cause are the characteristics of *dravya*.

[16] द्रव्याश्रय्यगुणवान् संयोगविभागेष्वकारणमनपेक्ष इति गुणलक्षणम् ॥ १६ ॥

dravyāśrayyaguṇavān saṁyogavibhāgeṣvakāraṇa-manapekṣa iti guṇalakṣaṇam ॥16 ॥

Residing in *dravya*, not possessing *guṇa*, and (when independent) not being a cause of contact or disjunction are the features of *guṇa*.

[17] एकद्रव्यमगुणं संयोगविभागेष्वानपेक्षकारणमिति कर्मलक्षणम् ॥ १७ ॥

ekadravyamaguṇaṁ saṁyogavibhāgeṣvānapekṣa-kāraṇamiti karmalakṣaṇam ॥17 ॥

(Residing at a time) in one *dravya*, (being) devoid of *guṇa* and (being) the unbiased independent cause of conjunction and disjunction, are the features of *karma*.

[18] द्रव्यगुणकर्मणां द्रव्यं कारणं सामान्यम् ॥ १८ ॥

dravyaguṇakarmaṇāṁ dravyaṁ kāraṇaṁ sāmānyam ॥18 ॥

Dravya is the common cause of *dravya, guṇa* and *karma*.

[19] तथा गुणः ॥ १९ ॥

tathā guṇaḥ ॥19 ॥

So is *guṇa* (too the common cause of *dravya, guṇa* and *karma*).

[20] संयोगविभागवेगानां कर्म समानम् ॥ २० ॥

saṁyogavibhāgavegānāṁ karma samānam ॥20 ॥

Karma is the common cause of conjunction, disjunction and motion.

[21] न द्रव्यानां कर्म ॥ २१ ॥

na dravyānāṁ karma ॥21 ॥

Karma is not (a cause) of *dravya.*

[22] व्यतिरेकात् ॥ २२ ॥

vyatirekāt ॥22 ॥

(Because) it is excluded (from them).

[23] द्रव्याणां द्रव्यं कार्यं सामान्यम् ॥ २३ ॥

dravyāṇāṁ dravyaṁ kāryaṁ sāmānyam ॥23 ॥

Dravya is the common effect of *dravyas.*

[24] गुणवैधर्म्यान्न कर्मणां कर्म ॥ २४ ॥

guṇavaidharmyānna karmaṇāṁ karma ॥24 ॥

Because of its dissimilarity from *guṇa, karma* is not (an effect) of *karmas.*

[25] द्वित्त्वप्रभृतयः संख्याः पृथक्त्वसंयोगविभागाश्च ॥ २५ ॥

dvittvaprabhṛtayaḥ saṅkhyāḥ pṛthaktvasaṁyoga-vibhāgāśca ॥24 ॥

(In *guṇas* like) numbers (which are) duality onwards, separateness, conjunction and disjunction (are generated by more than one *dravya*).

[26] असमवायात्सामान्यकार्यं कर्म न विद्यते ॥ २६ ॥

asamavāyātsāmānyakāryaṁ karma na vidyate ॥26 ॥

(Due to its) *asamavāya*[31] (in more than one *dravya*) *karma* is not the common effect (of several *dravyas*).

[27] संयोगानां द्रव्यम् ॥ २७ ॥

saṁyogānāṁ dravyam ॥27 ॥

---

31. Non-coinherence.

A *dravya* is (the effect) of conjunctions.

[28] रूपाणां रूपम् ॥ २८ ॥

rūpāṇāṁ rūpam ॥28 ॥

A colour/form is (the effect) of colours/forms.

[29] गुरुत्वप्रयत्नसंयोगानामुत्क्षेपनम् ॥ २९ ॥

gurutvaprayatnasaṁyogānāmutkṣepanam ॥29 ॥

(The *guṇa*) upward movement (is the effect) of heaviness, effort and contact.

[30] संयोगविभागाश्च कर्मणाम् ॥ ३० ॥

saṁyogavibhāgāśca karmaṇām ॥30 ॥

Conjunction and disjunction are also[32] (the effect) of *karma*.

[31] कारणसामान्ये द्रव्यकर्मणां कर्मकारणमुक्तम् ॥ ३१ ॥

kāraṇasāmānye dravyakarmaṇāṁ karmakāraṇa-muktam ॥31 ॥

In (the treatment of) cause in general, *karma* is not considered to be a cause of *dravya* and *karma*.

प्रथमोऽध्यायः प्रथम आह्निकम् समाप्तम् ॥

prathamo'dhyāyaḥ prathama āhnikam samāptam ॥

Thus ends the first *āhnika* of the first chapter.

---

32. *Ca* (also) here stands for motion. Conjunction, disjunction and motion are effects of *karma* (see 1.1.20).

द्वितीय आह्निक – Second Āhnika

Nature of Cause and Effect; Sāmānya and Viśeṣa

[32][33] कारणाभावात् कार्याभावः ॥ १ ॥

kārṇābhāvāt kāryābhāvaḥ ॥1 ॥

In the absence of cause is the absence of effect.

[33] न तु कार्याभावात् कारणाभावः ॥ २ ॥

na tu kāryābhāvāt kāraṇābhāvaḥ ॥2 ॥

But in the absence of effect there is no absence of cause.

[34] सामान्यं विशेष इति बुद्ध्यपेक्षम् ॥ ३ ॥

sāmānyaṁ viśeṣa iti buddhayapekṣam ॥ 3 ॥

(Both) *sāmānya* and *viśeṣa* depend upon the intellect.

Generality and Specificity in Dravya Guṇa and Karma

[35] भावोऽनुवृत्तेरेव हेतुत्वात् सामान्यमेव ॥ ४ ॥

bhāvo'nuvr̥ttereva hetutvāt sāmānyameva ॥4 ॥

Being/existence being the cause of continuity is *sāmānya*.

[36] द्रव्यत्वं गुणत्वं कर्मत्वं च सामान्यानि विशेषाश्च ॥ ५ ॥

dravyatvaṁ guṇatvaṁ karmatvaṁ ca sāmānyāni viśeṣāśca ॥5 ॥

Dravya, guṇa and *karma* are both *sāmānya* and *viśeṣa*.

---

33. The first number in parenthesis marks the continuous number of the *sūtra*, the number following the *sūtra* marks the *sūtra* number of that particular *āhnika*.

[37] अन्यत्रान्त्येभ्यो विशेषेभ्यः ॥ ६ ॥

anyatrāntyebhyo viśeṣebhyaḥ ॥6 ॥

Viśeṣa, being (the constituent of) ultimate differences, exists independent (of any percipient).

Definition of Sattā[34]

[38] सदिति यतो द्रव्यगुणकर्मसु सा सत्ता ॥ ७ ॥

saditi yato dravyaguṇakarmasu sā sattā ॥7 ॥

By which *dravya, guṇa* and *karma* appear to be existent, that is *sattā.*

Sattā in Dravya, Guṇa and Karma

[39] द्रव्यगुणकर्मभ्योऽर्थान्तरं सत्ता ॥ ८ ॥

dravyaguṇakarmabhyo'rthāntaraṁ sattā ॥ 8 ॥

Sattā is different from *dravya, guṇa,* and *karma.*

[40] गुणकर्मसु भावान्न कर्म न गुणः ॥ ९ ॥

guṇakarmaṣu bhāvānna karma na guṇaḥ ॥9 ॥

It is existent in *guṇa* and *karma* so it is neither *guṇa* nor *karma.*

[41] सामान्यविशेषाभावेन च ॥ १० ॥

sāmānyaviśeṣābhāvena ca ॥10 ॥

And also (because of the) non-presence of *sāmānya* and *viśeṣa* (*sattā* is different from others).

[42] अनेकमद्रव्यवत्त्वेन द्रव्यत्वमुक्तम् ॥ ११ ॥

anekadravyavattvena dravyatvamuktam ॥11 ॥

Dravyatva[35] is stated by its being in many *dravyas.*

34. Being, existence.

35. Thingness.

[43] सामान्यविशेषाभावेन च ॥ १२ ॥

sāmānyaviśeṣābhāvena ca ॥12 ॥

And also (because of the) non-presence of *sāmānya* and *viśeṣa*.

[44] तथा गुणेषु भावाद् गुणत्वमुक्तम् ॥ १३ ॥

tathā guṇeṣu bhāvād guṇatvamuktam ॥13 ॥

So is *guṇatva*[36] stated by its being in *guṇas*.

[45] सामान्यविशेषाभावेन च ॥ १४ ॥

sāmānyaviśeṣābhāvena ca ॥14 ॥

And also (because of the) non-presence of *sāmānya* and *viśeṣa*.

[46] कर्मसु भावात् कर्मत्वमुक्तम् ॥ १५ ॥

karmasu bhāvāt karmatvamuktam ॥15 ॥

Karmatva[37] is stated by its being in *karmas*.

[47] सामान्यविशेषाभावेन च ॥ १६ ॥

sāmānyaviśeṣābhāvena ca ॥ 16 ॥

And also (because of the) non-presence of *sāmānya* and *viśeṣa*.

[48] सदितिलिंगाविशेषाद् विशेषलिंगाभावच्चैको भावः ॥ १७ ॥

saditiliṅgāviśeṣād viśeṣaliṅgābhāvaccaiko bhāvaḥ ॥17 ॥

Sattā exists because of the non-particular mark of the being and the non-existence of the mark of *viśesa*.

प्रथमोऽध्यायः द्वितीयाह्निकम् समाप्तम् ॥

prathamo'dhyāyaḥ dvitīyāhnikaṁ samāptam ॥

End of first chapter — second *āhnika*.

36. Qualityness.
37. Actionness.

द्वितीय अध्याय – Second Chapter

प्रथम आह्निक – First Āhnika

Dravyas and Their Characteristics

[49] रूपरसगन्धस्पर्शवती पृथिवी ॥ १ ॥

rūparasagandhasparśavatī pṛthivī ॥1 ॥

(One which has) colour, taste, odour and touch is *pṛthivī.*

[50] रूपरसस्पर्शवत्य आपो द्रवाः स्निग्धाः ॥ २ ॥

rūparasasparśavatya āpo dravāḥ snigdhāḥ ॥2 ॥

(Having) colour, taste and touch, *āpa* is fluid and smooth.

[51] तेजोरूपस्पर्शवत् ॥ ३ ॥

tejorūpasparśavat ॥3 ॥

Teja has colour and touch.

[52] स्पर्शवान् वायुः ॥ ४ ॥

sparśavān vāyuḥ ॥4 ॥

Vāyu is touchable.

[53] त आकाशे न विद्यते ॥ ५ ॥

ta ākāśe na vidyate ॥5 ॥

These (*guṇas* namely colour, taste, odour and touch) are not present in *ākāśa.*

[54] सर्पिर्जतुमधूच्छिष्टानामग्निसंयोगाद् द्रवत्वमद्भिः सामान्यम् ॥ ६ ॥

sarpirjatumadhūcchiṣṭānāmagnisaṁyogād dravatvama-dbhiḥ sāmānyam ॥6 ॥

Butter, lac, beeswax, in contact with fire become (fluid, a property) common to (them and) water.

[55] त्रपुसीसलोहरजतसुवर्णानामग्निसंयोगाद् द्रवत्वमद्भिः सामान्यम् ॥ ७ ॥

trapusīsaloharajatasuvarṇānāmagnisaṁyogād dravatvamadbhiḥ sāmānyam ॥7 ॥

Tin, lead, iron, silver and gold, in contact with fire become (fluid, a property) common to (them and) water.

[56] विषाणी कुकुद्मान् प्रान्तेवालधिः सास्नावान् इति गोत्वे दृष्टं लिंगम् ॥ ८ ॥

viṣāṇī kukudvān prāntevāladhiḥ sāsnāvān iti gotve dṛṣtaṁ liṅgam ॥8 ॥

Horns, hump, hair at the tip of its tail, and a dewlap are the visible signs of a cow.

[57] स्पर्शश्च वायोः ॥ ९ ॥

sparśaśca vāyoḥ ॥9 ॥

(Similarly) touch (is the sign) of *vāyu* too.

[58] न च दृष्टानां स्पर्श इत्यदृष्टलिंगो वायुः ॥ १० ॥

na ca dṛṣṭānāṁ sparśa ityadṛṣṭaliṅgo vāyuḥ ॥10 ॥

And this touch is not of the visible (things), hence *vāyu* has an invisible mark.

[59] अद्रव्यवत्त्वेन द्रव्यम् ॥ ११ ॥

adravyavattvena dravyam ॥11 ॥

(*Vāyu* is) a *dravya* for not being (inherent) in other *dravya*s.

[60] क्रियावत्त्वाद् गुणत्त्ववाच्च ॥ १२ ॥

kriyāvattvād guṇattvavācca ॥12 ॥

And by possessing *kriyā*[38] and *guṇas* (*vāyu* is a *dravya*).

[61] अद्रव्यत्वेन नित्यत्वमुक्तम् ॥ १३ ॥

adravyatvena nityatvamuktam ॥13 ॥

(For) not being in other *dravyas* (*vāyu*) is stated to be *nitya.*[39]

[62] वायोर्वायुसम्मूर्च्छनं नानात्वे लिंगम् ॥ १४ ॥

vāyorvāyusammūrcchanaṁ nānātve liṅgam ॥14 ॥

The mixing of *vāyu* with *vāyu* is also the mark of its multiplicity.

[63] वायुसन्निकर्षे प्रत्यक्षाभावाद् दृष्टं लिंगं न विद्यते ॥ १५ ॥

vāyusannikarṣe pratyakṣābhāvād dṛṣṭaṁ liṅgaṁ na vidyate ॥15 ॥

(Since) the contact with *vāyu* is not perceptible there is no visible mark.

[64] सामान्यतो दृष्टाच्चाविशेषः ॥ १६ ॥

sāmānyato dṛṣṭāccāviśeṣaḥ ॥16 ॥

In the inference by general perception too (*vāyu*) is considered to be non-particular.

[65] तस्मादागमिकम् ॥ १७ ॥

tasmādāgamikam ॥17 ॥

Thus (the being of *vāyu*) has been handed down in the tradition.

---

38. Action.
39. Eternal, regular, lasting.

[66] संज्ञा कर्म त्वस्मद्विशिष्टानां लिंगम् ॥ १८ ॥

saṁjñā karma tvasmadviśiṣṭānāṁ liṅgam ॥18 ॥

(Just as) name and *karma* are marks of the particular distinguished things (similarly *vāyu* is known).

[67] प्रत्यक्षप्रवृत्तत्वात् संज्ञाकर्मणः ॥ १९ ॥

pratyakṣapravṛttatvāt saṁjñākarmaṇaḥ ॥19 ॥

(Because by) perception, name and *karma* are known to have been produced.

[68] निष्क्रमणं प्रवेशनमित्याकाशस्य लिंगम् ॥ २० ॥

niṣkramaṇaṁ praveśanamityākāśasya liṅgam ॥20 ॥

Exit and entry are the marks of *ākāśa.*

[69] तदलिंगमेक द्रव्यत्वात् कर्मणः ॥ २१ ॥

tadaliṅgameka dravyatvāt karmaṇaḥ ॥21 ॥

These (exit and entry) cannot be the mark (since) *karma* can inhere in (only) one *dravya.*

[70] कारणान्तरानुक्लृप्तिवैधर्म्याच्च ॥ २२ ॥

kāraṇāntarānuklṛptivaidharmyācca ॥22 ॥

And also because of its (*ākāśa*) difference from the marks of other causes.

[71] संयोगादऽभावः कर्मणः ॥ २३ ॥

saṁyogāda'bhāvaḥ karmaṇah ॥23 ॥

From conjunction (results) non-existence of *karma.*

[72] कारणगुणपूर्वकः कार्यगुणो दृष्टः ॥ २४ ॥

kāraṇaguṇapūrvakaḥ kāryaguṇo dṛṣṭaḥ ॥24 ॥

Before the *guṇa*s of the cause, the *guṇa*s of the effect are seen.

[73] कार्यन्तराप्रादुर्भावाच्च शब्दः स्पर्शवतमगुणः ॥ २५ ॥

kāryantarāprādurbhāvācca śabdaḥ sparśavatamaguṇaḥ ॥25 ॥

In the non-appearance of other effects too *śabda*[40] is not the *guṇa* of the tangible (entities).

[74] परत्र समवायात् प्रत्यक्षत्वाच्च नात्मगुणो न मनोगुणः ॥ २६ ॥

paratra samavāyāt pratyakṣatvācca nātmaguṇo na manoguṇaḥ ॥26 ॥

(Since it, *śabda,* is) inherent and perceived elsewhere (in other *dravya*s) it is neither the *guṇa* of *ātmā* nor of *mana.*

[75] परिशेषाल्लिंगमाकाशस्य ॥ २७ ॥

pariśeṣālliṅgamākāśasya ॥27 ॥

It remains that (sound) is a mark of *ākāśa.*

[76] द्रव्यत्वनित्यत्वे वायुना व्याख्यायते ॥ २८ ॥

dravyatvanityatve vāyunā vyākhyāyate ॥28 ॥

(Its) *dravyatva* and *nityatva*[41] is explained by *vāyu.*

[77] तत्त्वं भावेन ॥ २९ ॥

tattvaṁ bhāvena ॥29 ॥

Like being (existence) it is one.

[78] शब्दलिंगा विशेषाद्विशेषलिंगाभावाच्च ॥ ३० ॥

śabdaliṅgā viśeṣādviśeṣaliṅgābhāvācca ॥30 ॥

(Since) *śabda* as a mark is non-particular and due to the non-existence of other *viśeṣa* marks (of *ākāśa,* it is a unity).

---

40. Sound word.
41. Eternity, eternal nature.

[79] तदनुविधानादेकपृथक्त्वं चेति ॥ ३१ ॥

tadanuvidhānādekapṛthaktvaṁ ceti ॥31 ॥

Thus by this order (unity) it (*ākāśa*) is one and is also separate from others.

द्वितीयोऽध्यायः प्रथम आह्निकम् समाप्तम् ॥

dvitīyo'dhyāyaḥ prathama āhnikam samāptam ॥

Second Chapter — First *āhnika* ends here.

द्वितीय आह्निक – Second Āhnika

Examination of the Marks of the Dravyas

[80] पुष्पवस्त्रयोः सति सन्निकर्षे गुणान्तराप्रादुर्भावो वस्त्र गन्धाभा-वलिंगम् ॥ १ ॥

puṣpavastrayoḥ sati sannikarṣe guṇāntarāprādurbhāvo vastra gandhābhāvaliṅgam ॥1 ॥

(When) flower and cloth are brought close together, the non-appearance of the other *guṇa* in the cloth is the mark of non-presence of the odour (in the cloth).

[81] व्यवस्थितः पृथिव्यां गन्धः ॥ २ ॥

vyavasthitaḥ pṛthivyāṁ gandhaḥ ॥2 ॥

(It is) established that odour is (the mark) of *pṛthivī*.

[82] एतेनोष्णता व्याख्याता ॥ ३ ॥

etenoṣṇatā vyākhyātā ॥3 ॥

By this energy is explained.

[83] तेजस उष्णता ॥ ४ ॥

tejasa uṣṇatā ॥4 ॥

Energy is (the mark) of *teja*.

[84] अप्सु शीतता ॥ ५॥

apsu śītatā ॥5 ॥

Coldness is (the mark) of *āpa*.

[85] अपरस्मिन्नपरं युगपच्चिरं क्षिप्रमिति काललिंगानि ॥ ६ ॥

aparasminnaparaṁ yugapacciraṁ kṣipramiti kāla-liṅgāni ॥6 ॥

(The idea of) "posterior" (in relation to) that which is posterior simultaneity, slowness and quickness are the marks of *kāla*.

[86] तस्य द्रव्यत्वनित्यत्वे वायुना व्याख्याते ॥ ७ ॥

tasya dravyatvanityatve vāyunā vyākhyāte ॥7 ॥

Its *dravyatva* and *nityatva* is explained (as in) by *vāyu*.

[87] तत्त्वं भावेन ॥ ८ ॥

tattvaṁ bhāvena ॥8 ॥

Like being (existence) it is one.

[88] नित्येष्वभावादनित्येषु भावात् कारणे कालाख्येति ॥ ९ ॥

nityeṣvabhāvād anityeṣu bhāvāt kāraṇe kālākhyeti ॥9 ॥

(By) not being in *nitya* entities and being in *anitya* entities *kāla* is a (technical) term of the cause.

[89] इत इदमिति यतस्तद्दिश्यं लिंगम् ॥ १० ॥

ita idamiti yatastaddisyaṁ liṅgam ॥10 ॥

"This is in this side (direction)" such a (nature of) mark is of *diśā*.

[90] द्रव्यत्वनित्यत्वे वायुना व्याख्याते ॥ ११ ॥

dravyatvanityatve vāyuna vyākhyāte ॥11 ॥

(Its) *dravyatva* and *nityatva* is explained (as in) by *vāyu.*

[91] तत्त्वं भावेन ॥ १२ ॥

tattvaṁ bhāvena ॥12 ॥

Like being (existence) it is one.

[92] कार्यविशेषेण नानात्वम् ॥ १३ ॥

kāryaviśeṣeṇa nānātvam ॥13 ॥

By (nature of its) particular effects it (*diśā*) is many (diverse).

[93] आदित्यसंयोगाद् भूतपूर्वाद् भविष्यतो भूताच्च प्राची ॥ १४ ॥

ādityasaṁyogād bhūtapūrvād bhaviṣyato bhūtācca prācī ॥14 ॥

(*Diśā* is) regarded as (in the case of) East with its past, present and future relation to the sun.

[94] तथा दक्षिण प्रतीच्युदीची च ॥ १५ ॥

tathā dakṣiṇa pratīcyudīcī ca ॥15 ॥

So too is South, West and North (*diśā*s).

[95] एतेन दिगन्तरालानि व्याख्यातानि ॥ १६ ॥

etena digantarālāni vyākhyātāni ॥16 ॥

By this the other divisions of *diśā* explained.

Nature of Doubt

[96] सामान्यप्रत्यक्षाद् विशेषाप्रत्यक्षाद् विशेषस्मृतेश्च संशयः ॥ १७ ॥

sāmānyapratyakṣād viśeṣāpratyakṣād viśeṣasmṛteśca saṁśayaḥ ॥17 ॥

Perception of *sāmānya*, non-perception of *viśeṣa* and memory of *viśeṣa* raise doubt.

[97] दृष्टं च दृष्टवत् ॥ १८ ॥

dṛṣṭaṁ ca dṛṣṭavat ॥18 ॥

(That which is) seen and seen before (are causes of doubt).

[98] यथादृष्टमयथादृष्टत्वाच्च ॥ १९ ॥

yathādṛṣṭamayathādṛṣṭatvācca ॥19 ॥

(That which is) perceived in a way (in the past) thus not perceived similarly (at present) too (is a cause of doubt).

[99] विद्याविद्यातश्च संशयः ॥ २० ॥

vidyāvidyātaśca saṁśayaḥ ॥20 ॥

Knowledge and want of knowledge too (gives rise to) doubt.

Nature of Śabda

[100] श्रोत्रग्रहणोयोऽर्थः स शब्दः ॥ २१ ॥

śrotragrahaṇoyo'rthaḥ sa śabdaḥ ॥21 ॥

That (entity) which is apprehended by hearing is *śabda*.

[101] तुल्यजातीयेष्वर्थान्तरभूतेषु विशेषस्योभ यथा दृष्टत्वात् ॥ २२ ॥

tulyajātīyeṣvarthāntarabhūteṣu viśeṣasyobha yathā dṛṣṭatvāt ॥22 ॥

(Doubt arises because) a particular class of sound is perceived in both homogeneous and heterogeneous things.

[102] एकद्रव्यत्वान्नद्रव्यम् ॥ २३ ॥

ekadravyatvānnadravyam ॥23 ॥

(It) inheres in one *dravya* only, hence (*śabda* is) not a *dravya*.

[103] नापि कर्माचाक्षुषत्वात् ॥ २४ ॥

nāpi karmācākṣuṣatvāt ॥24 ॥

(It is) also not a *karma* since (it is) invisible.

[104] गुणस्य सतोऽपवर्गः कर्मभिः साधर्म्यम् ॥ २५ ॥

guṇasya sato'pavargaḥ karmabhiḥ sādharmyam ॥25 ॥

(Though) its (*śabda*'s) *guṇa* to end (transiency) is a common feature (which it shares) with *karma*.

[105] सतो लिंगाभावात् ॥ २६ ॥

sato liṅgābhāvāt ॥26 ॥

The mark of *sat* is absent (hence *śabda* is non-eternal).

[106] नित्यवैधर्म्यात् ॥ २७ ॥

nityavaidharmyāt ॥27 ॥

(It has) different *dharma* than the *nitya* (hence *śabda* is *anitya*, non-eternal).

[107] अनित्यश्चायं कारणतः ॥ २८ ॥

anityaścāyaṁ kāraṇataḥ ॥28 ॥

It is also *anitya* for it has a cause.

[108] न चासिद्धं विकारात् ॥ २९ ॥

na cāsiddhaṁ vikārāt ॥29 ॥

This (that *śabda* has a cause) is not unproved by change.

[109] अभिव्यक्तौ दोषात् ॥ ३० ॥

abhivyaktau doṣāt ॥30 ॥

In manifestation (lies the) fault (thus meaning is not proven; *śabda* is not manifested).

[110] संयोगाद् विभागाच्छब्दाच्च शब्दनिष्पत्तिः ॥ ३१ ॥

saṁyogād vibhāgācchabdācca śabdaniṣ-pattiḥ ॥31 ॥

Conjunction, disjunction and (other) *śabda*s give birth to *śabda*.

[111] लिंगाच्चानित्यः शब्दः ॥ ३२ ॥

liṅgāccānityaḥ śabdaḥ ॥32 ॥

Śabda is *anitya* too (because of) its mark.

Pūrvapakṣa[42]

[112] द्वयोस्तु प्रवृत्त्योरभावात् ॥ ३३ ॥

dvayostu pravr̥ttyorabhāvāt ॥33 ॥

(If *śabda* is *anitya* then) activities of both[43] would not exist.

[113] प्रथमाशब्दात् ॥ ३४ ॥

prathamāśabdāt ॥34 ॥

From the word *prathamā*.[44]

[114] सम्प्रतिपत्तिभावाच्च ॥ ३५ ॥

sampratipattibhāvācca ॥35 ॥

Also from the existence of recognition (and memory of what has been spoken in the past).

---

42. Possible arguments against what is established.

43. Of *guru* and *śiṣya* (teacher and student). If *śabda* is *anitya* the mode of oral teachings and similar reception would cease to exist.

44. In *R̥gveda*, 3.27.1 there are eleven *r̥cā*s (*śloka*s) mentioned of which the 'first' *r̥cā* (*prathamā*) is supposed to be recited thrice, thus if *śabda* were *anitya* this would not be possible.

Uttarapakṣa[45]

[115] सन्दिग्धः सति बहुत्वे ॥ ३६ ॥

saṁdigdhaḥ sati bahutve ॥36 ॥

All these arguments (for *śabda nityatva*) are doubtful.

[116] संख्याभावः सामान्यतः ॥ ३७ ॥

saṁkhyābhāvaḥ sāmānyataḥ ॥37 ॥

(As sounds) commonly exist (as) enumerable.

द्वितीयोऽध्यायः द्वितीयाह्निकम् समाप्तम् ॥

dvitīyo'dhyāyaḥ dvitīyāhnikam samāptam ॥

Thus ends the second *āhnika* of the second chapter.

45. Answering the argument to reestablish the already established statement.

तृतीय अध्याय – Third Chapter

प्रथम आह्निक – First Āhnika

Awareness of the Senses and Their Objects as the Marks of Proving the Existence of Ātmā

[117] प्रसिद्धा इन्द्रियार्थाः ॥ १ ॥

prasidhdā indriyārthāḥ ॥1 ॥

The objects of senses are well known.

[118] इन्द्रियार्थप्रसिद्धिरिन्द्रियार्थेभ्योऽर्थान्तरस्य हेतुः ॥ २ ॥

indriyārthaprasiddhirindriyārthebhyo'rthāntarasya hetuḥ ॥2 ॥

Cognition of senses and their objects is the mark of the existence of something other than senses and their objects.

[119] सोऽनपदेशः ॥ ३ ॥

so'napadeśaḥ ॥3 ॥

That (argument which says senses is of the body) is invalid.

[120] कारणाज्ञानात् ॥ ४ ॥

kāraṇājñānāt ॥4 ॥

(Because there is) no knowledge in cause.

[121] कार्येषु ज्ञानात् ॥ ५ ॥

kāryeṣu jñānāt ॥5 ॥

(And there would be) knowledge in effects.

[122] अज्ञानाच्च ॥ ६ ॥

ajñānācca ॥6 ॥

(And) also non-knowledge (of the presence of consciousness in matter).

Nature and Types of Proofs

[123] अन्यदेव हेतुरित्यनपदेशः ॥ ७ ॥

anyadeva heturityanapadeśaḥ ॥7 ॥

Another entity is the proof (of some other argument than the one supposed) hence (this too) is invalid.

[124] अर्थान्तरं ह्यर्थान्तरस्यानपदेशः ॥ ८ ॥

arthāntaraṁ hyarthāntarasyānapadeśaḥ ॥8 ॥

A different entity (or mark, as an argument) for yet another entity (which is wholly unconnected) is also not valid.

[125] संयोगिसमवाय्येकार्थसमवायिविरोधि च ॥ ९ ॥

saṁyogisamavāyyekārthasamavāyivirodhi ca ॥9 ॥

The conjunct, the inherent, the coinherence in one thing, and the contradictory (are the types of proof).

[126] कार्यं कार्यान्तरस्य ॥ १० ॥

kārya kāryāntarasya ॥10 ॥

An effect is (the mark of the existence) of another effect.

[127] विरोध्यभूतं भूतस्य ॥ ११ ॥

virodhyabhūtaṁ bhūtasya ॥11 ॥

A non-existent contradiction is (the mark) of the existent.

[128] भूतम भूतस्य ॥ १२ ॥

bhūtama bhūtasya ॥12 ॥

(That) which is, is (the mark of) that which is not.

[129] भूतो भूतस्य ॥ १३ ॥

bhūto bhūtasya ॥13 ॥

(That) which is, is (also the mark of) that which has been.

[130] प्रसिद्धिपूर्वकत्वादपदेशस्य ॥ १४ ॥

prasiddhipūrvakatvādapadeśasya ॥14 ॥

(These types of inferences are valid because) knowledge of the mark is preceded by existent knowledge.

Nature and Types of Fallacious Arguments

[131] अप्रसिद्धोऽनपदेशः ॥ १५ ॥

aprasiddho'napadeśaḥ ॥15 ॥

The unsubstantial is called fallacious (arguments).

[132] असन् संदिग्धश्चाऽनपदेशः ॥ १६ ॥

asan saṁdigdhaścā'napadeśaḥ ॥16 ॥

The unproven and the dubious are (the two types of) fallacious (arguments).

[133] यस्माद् विषाणी तस्मादश्वः ॥ १७ ॥

yasmād viṣāṇī tasmādaśvaḥ ॥17 ॥

Because it has horns thus it is a horse (is an example of the former type of fallacious argument).

[134] यस्माद् विषाणी तस्माद्गौरित्यनैकान्तिकस्योदाहरणम् ॥ १८ ॥

yasmād viṣāṇī tasmādgaurityanaikāntikasyodāharaṇam ॥18 ॥

Because it has horns it is a cow is an example of fallacy of plurality of consequents.

Existence of Other Ātmās

[135] आत्मेन्द्रियार्थसन्निकर्षाद्यन्निष्पद्यते तदन्यत् ॥ १९ ॥

ātmendriyārthasannikarṣādyanniṣpadyate tadanyat ॥19 ॥

That (knowledge) which is proven by the proximity of *ātmā* and the object of senses is different (from the fallacious).

[136] प्रवृत्तिनिवृत्ती च प्रत्यगात्मानि दृष्टे परत्र लिंगम् ॥ २० ॥

pravṛttinivṛttī ca pratyagātmāni dṛṣṭe paratra liṅgam ॥20 ॥

Activity and inactivity is seen in ones own *ātmā*, the mark is the same in others.

तृतीयोऽध्यायः प्रथमाह्निकम् समाप्तम् ॥

tritiyo'dhyāyaḥ prathamāhnikam samāptam ॥

Third chapter's first *āhnika* ends here.

द्वितीय आह्निक – Second Āhnika

Mana — Its Mark and Its Being a Dravya

[137] आत्मेन्द्रियार्थसन्निकर्षे ज्ञानस्य भावोऽभावश्च मनसो लिंगम् ॥ १ ॥

ātmendriyārthasannikarṣe jñānasya bhāvo'-bhāvaśca manaso liṅgam ॥1 ॥

(In cases of) proximity of *ātmā* and the objects of the senses, the existence and non-existence of knowledge is the mark of *mana*.

[138] तस्यद्रव्यत्वनित्यत्वे वायुना व्याख्याते ॥ २ ॥

tasya dravyatvanityatve vāyunā vyākhyāte ॥2 ॥

Its *dravyatva* and *nityatva* is explained (as in) by *vāyu*.

[139] प्रयत्नायौगपद्याज्ज्ञानायौगपद्याच्चैकम ॥ ३ ॥

prayatnāyaugapadyājjñānāyaugapadyāccaikama ॥3 ॥

(Because of) non-simultaneity of efforts and non-simultaneity of cognitions (it follows that) it (*mana*) is one (in every one).

Ātmā — Its Mark, Arguments for and against its Existence

[140] प्राणापाननिमेषोन्मेषजीवनमनोगतीन्द्रियान्तरविकाराः सुखदुःखेच्छाद्वेषप्रयत्नाश्चात्मनो लिंगानि ॥ ४ ॥

prāṇāpānanimeṣonmeṣajīvanamanogatīndriyāntaravikārāḥ sukhaduḥkhecchādveṣaprayatnāścātmano liṅgāni ॥4 ॥

Ascent and descent (of vital airs[46] opening and closing (of eyes), motions of life and *mana*, effects of the organs of sense, *sukha* and *duḥkha*, desire, aversion and effort are the marks of *ātmā*.

[141] तस्य द्रव्यत्वनित्यत्वे वायुना व्याख्याते ॥ ५ ॥

tasya dravyatvanityatve vāyunā vyākhyāte ॥5 ॥

Its *dravyatva* and *nityatva* is explained (as in) by *vāyu*.

[142] यज्ञदत्त इति सन्निकर्षे प्रत्यक्षाभावाद् दृष्टं लिंग न विद्यते ॥ ६ ॥

46. There are five vital airs, namely — *prāṇa* (breath/respiration), *apāna* (which descend and is released through the anus), *vyāna* (which circulates and is diffused throughout the body), *samāna* (which circulates about the hand and is essential to digestion) and *udāna* (one which is in the throat and rises upwards).

yajñadatta iti sannikarṣe pratykṣābhāvād dṛṣṭaṁ liṅgaṁ na vidyate ॥6 ॥

"This is Yajñadatta", (in this) there is absence of perception as there exists no visible marks (of his *ātmā*, even) in contact (of organs of sense and of cognition).

[143] सामान्यतोदृष्टाच्चाविशेषः ॥ ७ ॥

sāmānyatodṛṣṭāccāviśeṣaḥ ॥7 ॥

Based on *sāmānya* (generalised) perception (of observable signs) it cannot be inferred as *viśeṣa*.

[144] तस्मादागमिकः ॥ ८ ॥

tasmādāgamikaḥ ॥8 ॥

Thus it (the being of the *ātmā*) is proved (to exist) by the *āgama*.[47]

[145] अहमितिशब्दस्य व्यतिरेकान्नागमिकम् ॥ ९ ॥

ahamitiśabdasya veyatirekānnāgamikam ॥9 ॥

The word 'I' is different (in everyone, hence) the *āgama* is not the only proof.

[146] यदि दृष्टमन्वक्षमहं देवदत्तोऽहं यज्ञदत्त इति ॥ १० ॥

yadi dṛṣṭamanvakṣamahaṁ devadatto'haṁ yajñadatta iti ॥10 ॥

If the perception 'I am Devadatta, I am Yajñadatta' is seen (what is the need of inference?).

[147] दृष्ट आत्मनि लिङ्गे एक एव दृढ़त्वात् प्रत्यक्षवत् प्रत्ययः ॥ ११ ॥

dṛṣṭa ātmāni liṅge eka eva dṛḍhatvāt pratyakṣavat pratyayaḥ ॥11 ॥

---

47. Traditional doctrine, anything handed down and fixed by tradition, the Vedas.

If the mark of *ātmā* were seen, it would be an assurance (for it would be) then evident as a precept.

[148] देवदत्तो गच्छति यज्ञदत्तो गच्छतीत्युपचाराच्छरीरे प्रत्ययः ॥ १२ ॥

devdatto gacchati yajñadatto gacchatītyupacārā-ccharīre pratyayaḥ ॥12 ॥

"Devadatta goes, Yajñadatta goes" this could mean reference to the body.

[149] सन्दिग्धस्तूपचारः ॥ १३ ॥

sandigdhastūpacārāḥ ॥13 ॥

This application is doubtful.

[150] अहमिति प्रत्यगात्मानि भावात्परत्राभावादर्थान्तरप्रत्यक्षः ॥ १४ ॥

ahamiti pratyagātmāni bhāvātparatrābhāvādarthānta-rapratyakṣaḥ ॥14 ॥

The 'I' is cognised as a reference to each *ātmā* and (is a distinctive entity) not to any other, this difference is clearly seen.

[151] देवदत्तोगच्छतीत्युपचारादभिमानात्तावच्छरीर प्रत्यक्षोऽहंकारः ॥ १५ ॥

devdattogacchatītyupacārādabhimānāttāvaccharīr pratyakṣo'haṅkāraḥ ॥15 ॥

'Devatta goes', this application through the self-conscious expression shows that it ('I') is presentative of the body.

[152] सन्दिग्धस्तूपचारः ॥ १६ ॥

sandigdhastūpcāraḥ ॥16 ॥

This application is doubtful.

[153] न तु शरीरविशेषाद् यज्ञदत्तविष्णुमित्रयोर्ज्ञानं विषयः ॥ १७ ॥

na tu śarīraviśeṣād yajñadattaviṣṇu-mitrayorjñānaṁ viṣayaḥ ॥17 ॥

But the knowledge of Yajñadatta and Viṣṇumitra does not, due to their particular bodies become an object.

[154] अहमिति मुख्ययोग्याभ्यां शब्दवत् व्यतिरेकाव्यभिचाराद् विशेषसिद्धेर्नागमिकः ॥ १८ ॥

ahamiti mukhyayogyābhyāṁ śabdavat vyatirekāvya-bhicārād viśeṣasiddhernāgamikaḥ ॥18 ॥

The knowledge of the 'I', individually established by its predominant and sensible attributes does not depend on proof of the *āgama* alone for it is affirmed like *śabda* (by inference too).

[155] सुखदुःखज्ञाननिष्पत्त्यविशेषादैकात्मयम् ॥ १९ ॥

sukhaduḥkhajñānaniṣpattyaviśeṣādai-kātmayam ॥19 ॥

Due to the common origin of *sukha, duḥkha* and knowledge (in all bodies) *ātmā* is one.

[156] व्यवस्थातो नाना ॥ २० ॥

vyavasthāto nānā ॥20 ॥

(Because of) circumstances it (perception) is many (by special limitations as individuals).

[157] शास्त्रसामर्थ्याच्च ॥ २१ ॥

śāstrasāmarthyācca ॥21 ॥

And (so too) on the authority of the *śāstras*.

तृतीयोऽध्यायः द्वितीयाह्निकम् समाप्तम् ॥

tṛtīyo'dhyāyaḥ dvitīyāhnikam samāptam ॥

Thus ends the second *āhnika* of the third chapter.

चतुर्थ अध्याय – Fourth Chapter

प्रथम आह्निक – First Āhnika

Nityatā

[158] सदकारणवन्नित्यम् ॥ १ ॥

sadakāraṇavannityam ॥1 ॥

That (which is) eternal and uncaused is *nitya*.

[159] तस्य कार्यं लिङ्गम् ॥ २ ॥

tasya kāryaṁ liṅgam ॥2 ॥

Its effect is its mark.

[160] कारणभावात् कार्यभावः ॥ ३ ॥

kāraṇabhāvāt kāryabhāvaḥ ॥3 ॥

(From) existence of cause is existence of effect.

[161] अनित्य इति विशेषतः प्रतिषेधभावः ॥ ४ ॥

anitya iti viśeṣataḥ pratiṣedhabhāvaḥ ॥4 ॥

Anitya is the negation of existence of the *viśeṣa*.

[162] अविद्या ॥ ५ ॥

avidyā ॥5 ॥

(The supposition of *anityatā* only rises out of) ignorance.

Perception of Objects of Magnitude

[163] महत्यनेकद्रव्यवत्त्वाद् रूपाच्चोपलब्धिः ॥ ६ ॥

mahatyanekadravyavattvād rūpāccopalabdhiḥ ॥6 ॥

Perception is possible only of objects of magnitude (provided) they have more than one *dravya* and have colour/form.

[164] सत्यपि द्रव्यत्वे महत्त्वे रूपसंस्काराभावाद् वायोरनुपलब्धिः ॥ ७ ॥

satyapi dravyatve mahattve rūpasaṁskārābhāvād vāyoranupalabdhiḥ ॥7 ॥

Though a compound of many *dravya*s and being of substantial magnitude, *vāyu* is not perceptible because of the non-presence of colour.

Sensory Apperception as Knowledge

[165] अनेकद्रव्यसमवायाद् रूपविशेषाच्च रूपोपलब्धिः ॥ ८ ॥

anekadravyasamavāyād rūpaviśeṣācca rūpopa-labdhiḥ ॥8 ॥

Colour is perceived only when there is a particular colour or there is coinherence of more than one *dravya*.

[166] तेन रसगन्धस्पर्शेषु ज्ञानं व्याख्यातम् ॥ ९ ॥

tena rasagandhasparśeṣu jñānaṁ vyākhyātam ॥9 ॥

By this the cognition of taste, odour and touch, is explained.

[167] तस्याभावादव्यभिचारः ॥ १० ॥

tasyābhāvādavyabhicāraḥ ॥10 ॥

(In case of) its (taste, smell and touch) non-existence there will be no deviation.

[168] संख्याः परिमाणानि पृथकत्वं संयोगविभागौ परत्वापरत्वे कर्म च रूपिद्रव्यसमवायाच्चाक्षुषाणि ॥ ११ ॥

saṅkhyāḥ parimāṇāni pṛthakatvaṁ saṁyogavibhāgau paratvāparatve karma ca rūpidravyasamavāyā-ccākṣuṣāṇi ॥11 ॥

(The *guṇa*s) number, measure, separateness, conjunction, disjunction, otherness, non-otherness, and *karma* are visible to the eye (only if they) possess colour.

[169] अरूपिष्वचाक्षुषाणि ॥ १२ ॥

arūpiṣvacākṣuṣāṇi ॥12 ॥

In uncoloured (things) they (the *guṇa*s mentioned above) are not visible to the eye.

[170] एतेन गुणत्वे भावे च सर्वेन्द्रियं ज्ञानं व्याख्यातम् ॥ १३ ॥

etena guṇatve bhāve ca sarvendriyaṁ jñānaṁ vyākhyātām ॥13 ॥

By this the existence of the *guṇa*s and the cognition of all the senses is explained.

चतुर्थोऽध्यायः प्रथमाह्निकम् समाप्तम् ॥

caturtho'dhāyaḥ prathamāhnikam samāptam ॥

Fourth chapter — first *āhnika* ends here.

द्वितीय आह्निक – Second Āhnika

Nature, Composition and Types of Bodies

[171] तत् पुनः पृथिव्यादिकार्य्यद्रव्यं त्रिविधं शरीरेन्द्रियविषय संज्ञकम् ॥ १ ॥

tat punaḥ pṛthivyādikāryyadravyaṁ trividhaṁ śarīrendriyaviṣaya saṁjñakam ॥1 ॥

That again *pṛthivī*, etc., *dravya*s exist in three forms — body, sense and objects.

[172] प्रत्यक्षाप्रत्यक्षाणां संयोगस्याप्रत्यक्षत्वात् पञ्चात्मकं न विद्यते ॥ २ ॥

pratyakṣāpratyaksāṇāṁ saṁyogasyāpratyakṣatvāt pañcātmakaṁ na vidyate ॥2 ॥

(If) the conjunction of perceptible and imperceptible (*dravya*s) is not visible then it (body) is not the compound of five elements.

[173] गुणान्तराप्रादुर्भावाच्च ॥ ३ ॥

guṇāntarāprādurbhāvācca ॥3 ॥

(If) other *guṇa*s are unmanifested, then too (*pṛthvī*, etc., other effective *dravya*s cannot be considered as the compound of five).

[174] न त्र्यात्मकम् ॥ ४ ॥

na tryātmakam ॥4 ॥

Not of three elements (*pṛthvī, āpa* and *teja* — is body composed).

[175] अणुसंयोगस्त्वप्रतिषिद्धः ॥ ५ ॥

aṇusaṁyogastvapratiṣiddhaḥ ॥5 ॥

(Though a) conjunction of atoms is not denied.

[176] तत्र शरीरं द्विविधं योनिजमयोनिजं च ॥ ६ ॥

tatra śarīraṁ dvividhaṁ yonijamayonijaṁ ca ॥6 ॥

Of these bodies are of two types — *yonija*[48] and *ayonija*.[49]

---

48. Uterine — of mammals and born of eggs.
49. Non-uterine — of the first creatures, of the first men and born off the body, e.g., of sweat.

[177] अनियतदिग्देशपूर्वकत्वात् ॥ ७ ॥

aniyatadigdeśapūrvakatvāt ॥7 ॥

(Because early *ayonija* bodies) have antecedents in indeterminate time and space.

[178] धर्मविशेषाच्च ॥ ८ ॥

dharmaviśeṣācca ॥8 ॥

And (following) a particular *dharma*.

[179] समाख्याभावाच्च ॥ ९ ॥

samākhyābhāvācca ॥9 ॥

Also (because) linguistic evidence have existed.

[180] संज्ञाया अनादित्वात् ॥ १० ॥

saṁjñāyā anāditvāt ॥10 ॥

Since naming (or language) is without a beginning.

[181] सन्त्ययोनिजाः ॥ ११ ॥

santyayonijāḥ ॥11 ॥

(Thus) *ayonija* bodies exist.

[182] वेदलिङ्गाच्च ॥ १२ ॥

vedaliṅgācca ॥12 ॥

Also Vedas are the marker (proof).

चतुर्थोऽध्यायः द्वितीयाह्निकम् समाप्तम् ॥

caturtho'dhyāyaḥ dvitīyāhnikam samāptam ॥

Fourth chapter — second *āhnika* ends here.

पंचम अध्याय – Fifth Chapter

प्रथम आह्निक – First Āhnika

Description of Karma

[183] आत्मसंयोगप्रयत्नाभ्यां हस्ते कर्म ॥ १ ॥

ātmasaṁyogaprayatnābhyāṁ haste karma ॥1 ॥

The conjunction with and the effort of the *ātmā* results in the *karma* of the hand.

[184] तथा हस्तसंयोगाच्च मुसले कर्म ॥ २ ॥

tathā hastasaṁyogācca musale karma ॥2 ॥

Similarly, conjunction with the hand (and its being heavy) results in *karma* in the pestle.

[185] अभिघातजे मुसलादौ कर्मणि व्यतिरेकादकारणं हस्तसंयोगः ॥ ३ ॥

abhighātaje musalādau karmaṇi vyatirekāda-kāraṇaṁ hastasaṁyogaḥ ॥3 ॥

But, the *karma* (produced) in the pestle is due to the impact and not because of its conjunction with hand but otherwise (is seen even without the conjunction).

[186] तथात्मसंयोगो हस्तकर्मणि ॥ ४ ॥

tathātmasaṁyogo hastakarmaṇi ॥4 ॥

Similarly, conjunction of the *ātmā* (is not the cause of) *karma* in the hand.

[187] अभिघातान्मुसलसंयोगाद्धस्ते कर्म ॥ ५ ॥

abhighātānmusalasaṁyogāddhaste karma ॥5 ॥

Karma in the hand is due to the impact and conjunction with the pestle.

[188] आत्मकर्म हस्तसंयोगाच्च ॥ ६ ॥

ātmakarma hastasaṁyogācca ॥6 ॥

Karma of *ātmā* is also due to conjunction with the hand and (motion).

[189] संयोगाभावे गुरूत्वात् पतनम् ॥ ७ ॥

saṁyogābhāve gurutvāt patanam ॥7 ॥

In the non-presence of contact (the pestle) falls due to its heaviness.

[190] नोदनविशेषाभावान्नोर्ध्वं न तिर्य्यग्गमनम् ॥ ८ ॥

nodanaviśeṣābhāvānnordhavaṁ na tiryyaggamanam ॥8 ॥

(In the) absence of a paticular impulse the upward or sideward movement is not possible.

[191] प्रयत्नविशेषान्नोदनविशेषः ॥ ९ ॥

prayatnaviśeṣānnodanaviśeṣaḥ ॥9 ॥

From particular effort results particular impulse.

[192] नोदनविशेषादुदसनविशेषः ॥ १० ॥

nodanaviśeṣādudasanaviśeṣah ॥10 ॥

From particular impulse results the particular jumping (upwards).

[193] हस्तकर्मणा दारककर्म व्याख्यातम् ॥ ११ ॥

hastakarmaṇā dārakakarma vyākhyātam ॥11 ॥

By the *karma* of the hand the *karma* of a child is explained.

[194] तथा दग्धस्यविस्फोटने ॥ १२ ॥

tathā dagdhasyavisphoṭane ॥12 ॥

(And) so too, the bursting open of a burning object.

[195] यत्नाभावे प्रसुप्तस्य चलनम् ॥ १३ ॥

yatnābhāve prasuptasya calanam ॥13 ॥

In the absence of effort sleep-walking results.

[196] तृणे कर्म वायुसंयोगात् ॥ १४ ॥

tṛṇe karma vāyusaṁyogāt ॥14 ॥

Karma in the grass is due to its contact with *vāyu*.

[197] मणिगमनं सूच्यभिसर्पणमदृष्टकारणम् ॥ १५ ॥

maṇigamanaṁ sūcyabhisarpaṇamadṛṣṭakāraṇam ॥15 ॥

Movement of the gem (towards the thief), movement of the needle (towards the lodestone) are due to unseen causes.

[198] इषावयुगपत् संयोगविशेषाः कर्मान्यत्वे हेतुः ॥ १६ ॥

iṣāvayugapat saṁyogaviśeṣāḥ karmānyatve hetuḥ ॥16 ॥

In an arrow, many a time, particular conjunctions cause different *karma*.

[199] नोदनादाद्यमिषोः कर्म तत्कर्मकारिताच्च संस्कारादुत्तरं तथोत्तरमुत्तरञ्च ॥ १७ ॥

nodanādādyamiṣoḥ karma tatkarmakāritācca saṁskārāduttaraṁ tathottaramuttarañca ॥17 ॥

From impulse (results) the arrow's first *karma* the next from the inherent *saṁskāra*[50] which the arrow

50. Inherent tendencies, born within.

gains (from the first) and so on.

[200] संस्काराभावे गुरुत्वात् पतनम् ॥ १८ ॥

saṁskārābhāve gurutvāt patanam ॥18 ॥

The absence of *saṁskāra* and (the presence of) heaviness results in its (arrow's) fall (failing).

पंचमोऽध्यायः प्रथमाह्निकम् समाप्तम् ॥

pañcamo'dhyāyaḥ prathamāhnikam samāptam ॥

Here ends the first *āhnika* of the fifth chapter.

द्वितीय आह्निक – Second Āhnika

Karma in Dravyas due to Particular Impulse

[201] नोदनभिघातात् संयुक्तसंयोगाच्च पृथिव्यां कर्म ॥ १ ॥

nodanabhighātāt saṁyuktasaṁyogācca pr̥thivyāṁ karma ॥1 ॥

From the impact of impulse and united contact (of entities) results the *karma* in *pr̥thvī.*

[202] तद्विशेषेणादृष्टकारितम् ॥ २ ॥

tadviśeṣeṇādr̥ṣṭakāritam ॥2 ॥

These particulars are caused by unseen causes.

[203] अपां संयोगाभावे गुरूत्वात् पतनम् ॥ ३ ॥

apāṁ saṁyogābhāve gurutvāt patanam ॥3 ॥

Water falls due to absence of contact and due to (the presence) its heaviness.

[204] द्रवत्वात् स्यन्दनम् ॥ ४ ॥

dravatvāt syandanam ॥4 ॥

Fluidity (being the nature of liquids) results in flow.

[205] नोड़योवायुसंयोगादारोहणम् ॥ ५ ॥

noḍayovāyusaṁyogādārohaṇam ॥5 ॥

The rays of the sun in contact with *vāyu* (causes the) rise of water.

[206] नोदनपीडनात् संयुक्तसंयोगाच्च ॥ ६ ॥

nodanapīḍanāt saṁyuktasaṁyogācca ॥6 ॥

(Water rises up due to) the united contact, and the impulse of compression.

[207] वृक्षाभिसर्पणमित्यदृष्टकारितम् ॥ ७ ॥

vṛkṣābhisarpaṇamityadṛṣṭakāritam ॥7 ॥

Cirulation in tress is due to an unseen cause.

[208] अपां संघातो विलयनं च तेजः संयोगात् ॥ ८ ॥

apāṁ saṁghāto vilayanaṁ ca tejaḥ saṁyogāt ॥18 ॥

Freezing and melting of water, too is the result of its contact with *teja*.

[209] तत्र विस्फूर्जथुर्लिङ्गम् ॥ ९ ॥

tatra visphūrjathuraliṅgam ॥9 ॥

The mark (of the presence of *teja*) is the lightning and thunder.

[210] वैदिकं च ॥ १० ॥

vaidikaṁ ca ॥10 ॥

Also in Vedas (is it proved).

[211] अपां संयोगाद् विभागच्चस्तनयिनोः ॥ ११ ॥

apāṁ saṁyogād vibhāgaccastanayinoḥ ॥11 ॥

From the conjunction and disjunction of water (in the form of clouds) results lightning.

[212] पृथिवीकर्मणा तेजः कर्म वायुकर्म च व्याख्यातम् ॥ १२ ॥

pṛthivīkarmaṇā tejaḥ karma vāyukarma ca vyākhyātam ॥12 ॥

The *karma* of *teja* and *vāyu* are explained by the *karma* of *pṛthivī*.

[213] अग्नेरूर्ध्वज्वलनं वायोस्तिर्य्यक्पवनमणूनां मनसश्चाद्यं कर्मादृष्टकारितम् ॥ १३ ॥

agnerūrdhvajvalanaṁ vāyostiryyakpavanamaṇūnāṁ manasaścādyaṁ karmādṛṣṭakāritam ॥13 ॥

The upward flaming of fire, the sideward movement of *vāyu*, the first *karma* of atoms and *mana* are due to unseen causes.

[214] हस्तकर्मणा मनसः कर्म व्याख्यातम् ॥ १४ ॥

hastakarmaṇā manasaḥ karma vyākhyātam ॥14 ॥

The *karma* of the hand explains the *karma* of *mana*.

[215] आत्मेन्द्रियमनोर्थसन्निकर्षात् सुखदुःखे ॥ १५ ॥

ātmendriyamanorthasannikarṣāt sukhaduḥkhe ॥15 ॥

From the conjunction of *ātmā*, senses, *mana* and the object result *sukha* and *duḥkha*.

[216] तदनारम्भ आत्मस्थे मनसि शरीरस्य दुःखाभावः सः योगः ॥ १६ ॥

tadanārambha ātmasthe manasi śarīrasya duḥkhābhāvaḥ saḥ yogāḥ ॥16 ॥

When *mana* gets situated in the *ātmā* there is absense of its beginning (of *sukha-duḥkha*) then there is non-existence of *duḥkha* in the body, that is *yoga*.

[217] अपसर्पणमुपसर्पणमशितपीतसंयोगाः कार्यान्तरसंयोगाश्चेत्य-दृष्टकारितानि ॥ १७ ॥

apasarpaṇamupasarpaṇamaśitapītasaṁyogāḥ kāryāntarasaṁyogāścetyadr̥ṣṭakāritāni ॥17 ॥

The moving away and coming closer (of the *manas* to the *ātmā*), conjunctions of things eaten and drunk and conjunctions with all other effects, (all these) are done by unseen causes.

[218] तदभावे संयोगाभावोऽप्रादुर्भावश्च मोक्षः ॥ १८ ॥

tadabhāve saṁyogābhāvo'prādurbhāvaśca mokṣaḥ ॥18 ॥

When there is non-existence of this (*adr̥ṣṭa*), there is non-existence of conjunction and non-existence of manifestation that is *mokṣa.*

[219] द्रव्यगुणकर्मनिष्पत्तिवैधर्म्यादभावस्तमः ॥ १९ ॥

dravyaguṇakarmaniṣpattivaidharmyādabhāva-stamaḥ ॥19 ॥

Darkness is a non-presence being dissimilar to the production of *dravya, guṇa* and *karma.*

[220] तेजसो द्रव्यान्तरेणावरणाच्च ॥ २० ॥

tejaso dravyāntareṇāvaraṇācca ॥20 ॥

And because of the obscuring of *teja* (light) by other *dravya.*

[221] दिक्कालावकाश च क्रियावद्वैधर्म्यात् निष्क्रियाणि ॥ २१ ॥

dikkālāvakāśaṁ ca kriyāvadvaidharmyāt niṣkriyāṇi ॥21 ॥

Diśā, kāla and *ākāśa* are also opposed to action thus they are non-dynamic.

[222] एतेन कर्माणि गुणाश्च व्याख्याताः ॥ २२ ॥

etena karmāṇi guṇāśca vyākhyātāḥ ॥22 ॥

By this are explained *karma* and *guṇa.*

[223] निष्क्रियाणां समवायः कर्मभ्यो निषिद्धः ॥ २३ ॥

niṣkriyāṇāṁ samavāyaḥ karmabhyo niṣiddhaḥ ॥23 ॥

The coinherence of non-dynamic things is excluded from *karma.*

[224] कारणं त्वऽसमवायिनो गुणाः ॥ २४ ॥

kāraṇam tva'samavāyino guṇāḥ ॥24 ॥

(But) *guṇa*s as a cause (of *karma*) are non-co-inherent.

[225] गुणैर्दिग्व्याख्याता ॥ २५ ॥

guṇairdigvyākhyātā ॥25 ॥

By *guṇa diśā* is explained.

[226] कारणेन कालः ॥ २६ ॥

kāraṇena kālaḥ ॥26 ॥

By cause time (is explained).

पंचमोऽध्यायः द्वितीयाह्निकम् समाप्तम् ॥

pañcamo'dhyāyaḥ dvitīyāhnikam samāptam ॥

Here ends the second *āhnika* of the fifth chapter.

षष्ठम अध्याय – Sixth Chapter

प्रथम आह्निक – First Āhnika

Concepts of Dāna,[51] Pratigraha[52] and Tyāga[53]

[227] बुद्धिपूर्वा वाक्यकृतिर्वेदे ॥ १ ॥

buddhipūrvā vākyakṛtirvede ॥1 ॥

The statements of Vedas are created knowledgeably.

[228] ब्राह्मणे संज्ञाकर्म सिद्धिलिङ्गम् ॥ २ ॥

brāhmaṇe saṁjñākarma siddhiliṅgam ॥2 ॥

Names and *guṇa*s in the *Brāhmaṇa*s are the mark of that.

[229] बुद्धिपूर्वो ददातिः ॥ ३ ॥

budhdipūrvo dadātiḥ ॥3 ॥

Giving is wise.

[230] तथा प्रतिग्रहः ॥ ४ ॥

tathā pratigrahaḥ ॥4 ॥

And so is receiving.

[231] आत्मान्तरगुणानामात्मान्तरेऽकारणत्वात् ॥ ५ ॥

---

51. Giving, alms.
52. Receiving.
53. Renunciation.

ātmāntaraguṇānāmātmāntare'kāraṇatvāt ॥5॥

(Because) the *guṇa* of one *ātmā* is not a cause with regard to another *ātmā*.

[232] तद् दुष्टभोजने न विद्यते ॥ ६ ॥

tad duṣṭabhojane na vidyate ॥6॥

That (wisdom) is not present in impure food.

[233] दुष्टं हिंसायाम् ॥ ७ ॥

duṣṭaṁ hiṁsāyām ॥7॥

In impurity is *hiṁsā*.[54]

[234] तस्य समभिव्याहारतो दोषः ॥ ८ ॥

tasya samabhivyāhārato doṣaḥ ॥8॥

Association with it results in *doṣa*.[55]

[235] तददुष्टे न विद्यते ॥ ९ ॥

tadduṣṭe na vidyate ॥9॥

Tḥat is not present in the non-impure.

[236] पुनर्विशिष्टे प्रवृत्तिः ॥ १० ॥

punarviśiṣṭe pravṛttiḥ ॥10॥

Again relation should be maintained with the superiors.

[237] समे हीने वा प्रवृत्ति ॥ ११ ॥

same hīne vā pravṛtti ॥11॥

And with (those) similar and low (in stature).

[238] एतेन हीनसमविशिष्टधार्मिकेभ्यः परस्वादानं व्याख्यातम् ॥ १२ ॥

---

54. Violence, hatred.
55. Flaw, demerit.

etena hīnasamaviśiṣṭadhārmikebhyaḥ parasvādānaṁ vyākhyātam ॥12 ॥

By this the (nature of) reception among one another who are of the nature of superior, similar and low is explained.

[239] तथा विरुद्धानां त्यागः ॥ १३ ॥

tathā viruddhānāṁ tyāgaḥ ॥13 ॥

And apposed to this (receiving) is *tyāga*.

[240] हीने परे त्यागः ॥ १४ ॥

hīne pare tyāgaḥ ॥14 ॥

Give up the low.

[241] समे आत्मत्यागः परत्यागो वा ॥ १५ ॥

same ātmatyāgaḥ paratyāgo vā ॥15 ॥

For the similar give up the self or give them up.

[242] विशिष्टे आत्मत्याग इति ॥ १६ ॥

viśiṣṭe ātmatyāga iti ॥16 ॥

To the superior give up the self.

षष्ठोऽध्यायः प्रथमाह्निकम् समाप्तम् ॥

ṣaṣṭho'dhyāyaḥ prathamāhnikam samāptam ॥

Thus end the first *āhnika* of the sixth chapter.

द्वितीय आह्निक – Second Āhnika

On Seen and Unseen Deeds Which Produce Merit

[243] दृष्टादृष्टप्रयोजनानां दृष्टाभावे प्रयोजनमभ्युदाय ॥ १ ॥

dṛṣṭādṛṣṭaprayojanānāṁ dṛṣṭābhāve prayojana-mabhyudāya ॥1 ॥

Actions of motives are seen or unseen, where it is unseen tends to *abhyudaya*.[56]

[244] अभिषेचनोपवासब्रह्मचर्यगुरुकुलवासवान प्रस्थयज्ञदानप्रोक्षणदिङ्नक्षत्र मन्त्रकालनियमाश्चादृष्टाय ॥ २ ॥

abhiṣecanopavāsabrahmacaryagurukulavāsavāna prasthayajñadānaprokṣaṇadiññakṣatra mantrakāla-niyamāścādṛṣṭāya ॥2 ॥

Fasting, continence, residence in the *gurukula*,[57] life in the forest, giving, oblation, knowing the *diśā*s and the constellations, incantation of sacred texts and following the seasons and observances of religion conduce to invisible result.

Activities of Anupadhā[58] that Produce Merit

[245] चतुराश्रम्यमुपधा अनुपधाश्च ॥ ३ ॥

caturāśramyamupdhā anupadhāśca ॥3 ॥

The duties of the four *āśramas*[59] of life are rooted in *anupadhā* and *upadhā*.

[246] भावदोष उपधाऽदोषोऽनुपधा ॥ ४ ॥

bhāvadoṣa upadhā'doṣo'nupadhā ॥4 ॥

Deficiency of faith is an *upadhā* and non-deficiency is an *anupadhā*.

[247] यदिष्टरूपरसगन्धस्पर्शं प्रोक्षितमभ्युक्षितञ्चतच्छुचि ॥ ५ ॥

yadiṣṭarūparasagandhasparśaṁ prokṣitamabhyukṣita-ñcatacchuci ॥5 ॥

---

56. Exaltation.
57. Teacher's *āśrama* (home).
58. Fidelity.
59. *Brahmacarya* (the bachelor student), *gṛhastha* (familyman), *vānaprastha* (forest dwelling) and *sanyāsa* (becoming a mendicant).

That which is of the prescribed colour, taste, odour and touch, which is oblated upon and sprinkled with water is pure.

[248] अशुचीति शुचिप्रतिषेधः ॥ ६ ॥

aśucīti śucipratiṣedhaḥ ॥6 ॥

Impurity is the negation of purity.

[249] अर्थान्तरञ्च ॥ ७ ॥

arthāntarañca ॥7 ॥

Different from the prescribed object (too is impure).

[250] अयतस्य शुचिभोजनादभ्युदयो न विद्यते नियमाभावात् ॥ ८ ॥

ayatasya sucibhojanādabhyudayo na vidyate niyamābhāvāt ॥8 ॥

Even partaking pure food without following the prescriptions will result in absence of *abhyudaya*.

[251] विद्यते वाऽर्थान्तरत्वात् यमस्य ॥ ९ ॥

vidyate vā'rthāntaratvāt yamasya ॥9 ॥

Or it occurs because restraint means something else.

[252] असति चाभावात् ॥ १० ॥

asati cābhāvāt ॥10 ॥

There is non-existence where it is not.

[253] सुखाद् रागः ॥ ११ ॥

sukhād rāgaḥ ॥11 ॥

From pleasure arises desire.

[254] तन्मयत्वाच्च ॥ १२ ॥

tanmayatvācca ॥12 ॥

Also through that being engrained.

[255] अदृष्टाच्च ॥ १३ ॥

adṛṣṭācca ॥13 ॥

Due to the unseen.

[256] जातिविशेषाच्च ॥ १४ ॥

jātiviśeṣācca ॥14 ॥

Also due to particularity of natures.

[257] इच्छाद्वेषपूर्विका धर्माधर्मप्रवृत्तिः ॥ १५ ॥

icchādveṣapūrvikā dharmādharma-pravṛttiḥ ॥15 ॥

Due to desire or aversion man performs *dharma* or *adharma*.

[258] तत् संयोगो विभागः ॥ १६ ॥

tat saṁyogo vibhāgaḥ ॥16 ॥

By these are conjunction and disjunction (explained).

[259] आत्मकर्मसु मोक्षो व्याख्यातः ॥ १७ ॥

ātmakarmasu mokṣo vyākhyātaḥ ॥17 ॥

Mokṣa is explained as being dependent on the *karma* of the *ātmā*.

षष्ठोऽध्यायः द्वितीयाह्निकम् समाप्तम् ॥

ṣaṣṭho'dhyāyaḥ dvitīyāhnikam samāptam ॥

Sixth chapter second *āhnika* ends here.

सप्तम अध्याय – Seventh Chapter

प्रथम आह्निक – First Āhnika

Nitya and Anitya Guṇas

[260] उक्ता गुणाः ॥ १ ॥

uktā guṇāḥ ॥1 ॥

*Guṇa*s have been stated.

[261] पृथिव्यादिरूपरसगन्धस्पर्शा द्रव्यनित्यत्वादनित्याश्च ॥ २ ॥

pṛthivyādirūparasagandhasparśā dravyanityatvādanityāśca ॥2 ॥

The colour, taste, odour and touch of *pṛthivī*, etc., are *anitya* (since they are) *anitya dravya*s.

[262] एतेन नित्येषु नित्यत्वमुक्तम् ॥ ३ ॥

etena nityeṣu nityatvamuktam ॥3 ॥

By this is said the *nityatva* in *nitya* things.

[263] अप्सु तेजसि वायौ च नित्या द्रव्यनित्यत्वात् ॥ ४ ॥

apsu tejasi vāyau ca nityā dravyanityatvāt ॥4 ॥

They (the *guṇa*s) are *nitya* in *āp*, *teja* and *vāyu* as they (the *dravya*s) are *nitya*.

[264] अनित्येष्वनित्या द्रव्यानित्यत्वात् ॥ ५ ॥

anityeṣvanityā dravyānityatvāt ॥5 ॥

In things *anitya* they (the *guṇa*s) are *anitya* as the *dravya*s are *anitya*.

[265] कारणगुणपूर्वकाः पृथिव्यां पाकजाः ॥ ६ ॥

kāraṇaguṇapūrvakāḥ pṛthivyāṁ pākjāḥ ॥6 ॥

The change of *guṇa*s produced by heat in *pṛthivī* has its beginning in the cause.

[266] एकद्रव्यत्वात् ॥ ७ ॥

ekadravyatvāt ॥7 ॥

(Because there is) one *dravya* only.

Aṇutva[60] and Mahattva[61]

[267] अणोर्महतश्चोपलध्यनुपलब्धी नित्ये व्याख्याते ॥ ८ ॥

aṇormahataścopaladhyanupalabdhī nitye vyākhyāte ॥8 ॥

The perception and non-perception of *aṇu* and *mahat* has been explained to be *nitya.*

[268] कारणबहुत्वाच्च ॥ ९ ॥

kāraṇabahutvācca ॥9 ॥

In consequence of plurality too (*mahat* is produced).

[269] अतो विपरीतमणु ॥ १० ॥

ato viparītamaṇu ॥10 ॥

Its opposite is an *aṇu.*

[270] अणु महदिति तस्मिन् विशेषभावात् विशेषाभावाच्च ॥ ११ ॥

aṇu mahaditi tasmin viśeṣabhāvāt viśeṣābhāvācca ॥11 ॥

The notions of greater and smaller size are said to be relative on the existence or non-existence of *viśeṣa.*

---

60. Atomicity.
61. Magnitude.

[271] एककालत्वात् ॥ १२ ॥

ekakālatvāt ॥12 ॥

(Because there is) one time.

[272] दृष्टान्ताच्च ॥ १३ ॥

dṛṣṭāntācca ॥13 ॥

Examples too can be given.

[273] अणुत्वमहत्त्वयोरणुत्वमहत्त्वाऽभावः कर्मगुणैर्व्याख्यातः ॥ १४ ॥

aṇutvamahattvayoraṇutvamahattvā'bhāvaḥ karmaguṇa-irvyākhyātaḥ ॥14 ॥

The non-existence of *aṇutva* and *mahattva* in *aṇutva* and *mahattva* is explained in *karma* and *guṇa*.

[274] कर्मभिः कर्माणि गुणैश्च गुणा व्याख्याताः ॥ १५ ॥

karmabhiḥ karmāṇi guṇaiśca guṇā vyākhyātāḥ ॥15 ॥

By *karmas karma* and by *guṇas guṇa* has been explained.

[275] अणुत्वमहत्त्वाभ्यां कर्मगुणाश्च व्याख्याताः ॥ १६ ॥

aṇutvamahattvābhyāṁ karmaguṇāśca vyākhyātāḥ ॥16 ॥

And also by *aṇutva* and *mahattva karma* and *guṇa* are explained.

[276] एतेन दीर्घत्वह्रस्वत्वे व्याख्याते ॥ १७ ॥

etena dīrghatvahrasvatve vyākhyāte ॥17 ॥

By this the notions of length and shortness are explained.

[277] अनित्येऽनित्यम् ॥ १८ ॥

anitye'nityam ॥18 ॥

In *anitya* (*dravya*s) these (four categories) are *anitya*.

[278] नित्ये नित्यम् ॥ १९ ॥

nitye nityam ॥19 ॥

In *nitya* (*dravyas*, these notions are) *nitya*.

[279] नित्यं परिमण्डलम् ॥ २० ॥

nityaṁ parimaṇḍalam ॥20 ॥

The roundness (of atom) is *nitya*.

[280] अविद्या च विद्यालिंगम् ॥ २१ ॥

avidyā ca vidyāliṅgam ॥21 ॥

Ignorance is also the marker of knowledge.

Size of Ākāśa, Mana, Diśā and Kāla

[281] विभावान्महानाकशस्तथा चात्मा ॥ २२ ॥

vibhāvānmahānākaśastathā cātmā ॥22 ॥

Ākāśa and *ātmā* by merit of their size are called pervasive.

[282] तदभावादणुमनः ॥ २३ ॥

tadabhāvādaṇumanaḥ ॥23 ॥

In (consequence of) non-presence of that (pervasiveness) *mana* is small.

[283] गुणैर्दिग्व्याख्याता ॥ २४ ॥

guṇairdigvyākhyātā ॥24 ॥

By *guṇas*, *diśā* is explained.

[284] कारणे कालः ॥ २५ ॥

kāraṇe kālaḥ ॥25 ॥

By cause (is explained) *kāla*.

सप्तमोऽध्यायः प्रथमाह्निकम् समाप्तम् ॥

saptamo'dhyāyaḥ prathamāhnikam samāptam ॥

Seventh chapter first *āhnika* ends thus.

द्वितीय आह्निक – Second Āhnika

Ekatva[62] and Pṛthaktva[63]

[285] रूपरसगन्धस्पर्शव्यतिरेकादर्थान्तरमेकत्वम् ॥ १ ॥

rūparasagandhasparśavyatirekādarthāntaramekatvam ॥1 ॥

(By being) distinct from colour, taste, odour and touch, *ekatva* is a different entity.

[286] तथा पृथक्त्वम ॥ २ ॥

tathā pṛthaktvam ॥2 ॥

Similarly, *pṛthaktva*.

[287] एकत्वैकपृथक्त्वयोरेकत्वैकपृथक्त्वाभावोऽणुत्वमहत्त्वाभ्यां व्याख्यातः ॥ ३ ॥

ekatvaikapṛthaktvayorekatvaikapṛthaktvābhāvo'-ṇutvamahattvābhyāṁ vyākhyātaḥ ॥3 ॥

The non-existence of *ekatva* and *pṛthaktva* in *ekatva* and *pṛthaktva* is explained by *aṇutva* and *mahattva*.

[288] निःसंख्यत्वात्कर्मगुणानां सर्वैकत्वं न विद्यते ॥ ४ ॥

niḥsaṅkhyatvātkarmaguṇānāṁ sarvaikatvaṁ na vidyate ॥4 ॥

Ekatva does not exist in all things for *karma* and *guṇa* are non-numbered.

[289] भ्रान्तं तत् ॥ ५ ॥

bhrāntaṁ tat ॥5 ॥

That (notion) is wrong.

[290] एकत्वाभावाद् भक्तिस्तु न विद्यते ॥ ६ ॥

ekatvābhāvād bhaktistu na vidyate ॥6 ॥

---

62. Unity, similarity.
63. Distinctiveness, separateness, duality.

In non-existence of *ekatva* secondariness does not exist.

[291] कार्यकारणयोरेकत्वैकपृथक्त्वाभावादेकत्वैकपृथक्त्वं न विद्यते ॥ ७ ॥

kāryakāraṇayorekatvaikapṛthaktvābhāvādekatvaika-pṛthaktvaṁ na vidyate ॥7 ॥

Of cause and effect there is no *ekatva* and *pṛthaktva* in consequence of the non-existence of *ekatva* and *pṛthaktva.*

[292] एतदनित्ययोर्व्याख्यातम् ॥ ८ ॥

etadanityayorvyākhyātam ॥8 ॥

This is explained in relation to the *anitya* (cause and effect).

Conjunction and Disjunction

[293] अन्यतरकर्मजः उभयकर्मजः संयोगश्चसंयोगः ॥९ ॥

anyatarakarmajaḥ ubhayakarmajaḥ saṁyogaśca-saṁyogaḥ ॥9 ॥

A conjunct is produced by the *karma* of one of the two, by the *karma* of both or by conjunction.

[294] एतेन विभागो व्याख्यातः ॥ १० ॥

etena vibhāgo vyākhyātaḥ ॥10 ॥

By this disjunction is explained.

[295] संयोगविभागयोः संयोगविभागाभावोऽणुत्वमहत्त्वाभ्यां व्याख्यातः ॥ ११ ॥

saṁyogavibhāgayoḥ saṁyogavibhāgābhāvo' ṇutva mahattvābhyāṁ vyākhyātaḥ ॥11 ॥

The non-existence of conjunction and disjunction in conjunction and disjunction is explamed by *aṇutva* and *mahattva*.

[296] कर्मभिः कर्माणि गुणैश्च गुणाः अणुत्वमहत्त्वाभ्यामिति ॥ १२ ॥

karmabhiḥ karmāṇi guṇaiśca guṇāḥ aṇutvamahattvābhyāmiti ॥12 ॥

*Karma*s in *karma* and *guṇa*s in *guṇa* is explained (earlier) by *aṇutva* and *mahattva*.

[297] युतसिद्धयभावात् कार्यकारणयोः संयोगविभागौ न विद्येते ॥ १३ ॥

yutasiddhayabhāvāt kāryakāraṇayoḥ saṁyoga-vibhāgau na vidyete ॥13 ॥

There is neither conjunction or disjunction in cause and effect since they do not exist independently.

[298] गुणत्वात् ॥ १४ ॥

guṇatvāt ॥14 ॥

As it is a *guṇa*.

[299] गुणोऽपि विभाव्यते ॥ १५ ॥

guṇo'pi vibhāvyate ॥15 ॥

Guṇa is also implied.

[300] निष्क्रियत्वात् ॥ १६ ॥

niṣkriyatvāt ॥16 ॥

As there is no action (thus no conjunction or disjunction).

[301] असति नास्तीति च प्रयोग्यात् ॥ १७ ॥

asati nāstīti ca prayogyāt ॥17 ॥

Also the expression of 'it is not' is used (in case of the non-existent).

[302] शब्दार्थवसम्बन्धौ ॥ १८ ॥

śabdārthavasambandhau ॥18 ॥

(Thus) the *śabda* and its meaning is without connection.

[303] संयोगिनो दण्डात् समवायिनो विशेषाच्च ॥ १९ ॥

saṁyogino daṇḍāt samavāyino viśeṣācca ॥19 ॥

(Cognition of) that which is a conjunction (results from the knowledge of the conjunct, for example) contact with a staff (and cognition of that) which possesses co-inhesion from the particular.

[304] सामयिकः शब्दार्थप्रत्ययः ॥ २० ॥

sāmayikaḥ śabdārthapratyayaḥ ॥20 ॥

Relation between the *śabda* and its meaning is significatory.

Otherness and Non-Otherness

[305] एकदिक्काभ्यामेककालाभ्यां सन्निकृष्टविप्रकृष्टाभ्यां परमपरञ्च ॥ २१ ॥

ekadikkābhyāmekakālābhyāṁ sannikṛṣṭavipra-kṛṣṭābhyaṁ paramaparañca ॥21 ॥

Otherness and non-otherness is (explained) by nearness and farness of objects residing in the same place at the same time.

[306] कारणपरत्वात् कारणापरत्वाच्च ॥ २२ ॥

kāraṇaparatvāt kāraṇāparatvācca ॥22 ॥

From the closeness of cause otherness and from the farness of cause non-otherness (results).

[307] परत्वापरत्वयोः परत्वापरत्वाभावोऽणुत्वमहत्त्वाभ्यां व्याख्यातः ॥ २३ ॥

paratvāparatvayoḥ pratvāparatvābhāvo'-ṇutvamahattvābhyaṁ vyākhyātaḥ ॥22 ॥

The non-existence of otherness and non-otherness in otherness and non-otherness is explained by *aṇutva* and *mahattva*.

[308] कर्मभिः कर्माणि ॥ २४ ॥

karmabhiḥ karmāṇi ॥24 ॥

(As) *karmas* is *karma* (is said earlier).

[309] गुणैर्गुणाः ॥ २५ ॥

guṇairguṇāḥ ॥25 ॥

(As) *guṇas* in *guṇa* (has been explained in relation to *aṇutva* and *mahattva*).

Samavāyaḥ as a Dravya

[310] इहेदमिति यतः कार्यकारणयोः स समवायः ॥ २६ ॥

ihedamiti yataḥ kāryakāraṇayoḥ sa samavāyaḥ ॥26 ॥

Samavāya is that by the virtue of which cause and effect may be said to be in one another.

[311] द्रव्यत्वगुणत्वप्रतिषेधो भावेन व्याख्यातः ॥ २७ ॥

dravyatvaguṇatvapratiṣedho bhāvena vyākhyātaḥ ॥27 ॥

The negation of the essence of *dravyatva* and *guṇatva* is explained by (its) existence.

[312] तत्त्वं भावेन ॥ २८ ॥

tattvaṁ bhāvena ॥28 ॥

Its truth is (explained by) existence.

सप्तमोऽध्यायः द्वितीयाह्निकम् समाप्तम् ॥

saptamo'dhyāyaḥ dvitīyāhnikam samāptam ॥

Seventh chapter second *āhnika* ends here.

अष्टम अध्याय – Eighth Chapter

प्रथम आह्निक – First Āhnika

Examination of Cognition

[313] द्रव्येषु ज्ञानं व्याख्यातम् ॥ १ ॥

dravyeṣu jñānaṁ vyākhyātam ॥1 ॥

Cognition was explained in (chapter of) *dravyas*.

[314] तत्रात्मा मनश्चाप्रत्यक्षे ॥ २ ॥

tatrātmā manaścāpratyakṣe ॥2 ॥

In them *ātmā* and *mana* are not visible.

[315] ज्ञाननिर्देशे ज्ञाननिष्पत्तिविधिरुक्तः ॥ ३ ॥

jñānanirdeśe jñānaniṣpattividhiruktaḥ ॥3 ॥

The mode of origin of cognition has been stated in the enunciation of cognition.

[316] गुणकर्मसु सन्निकृष्टेषु ज्ञाननिष्पत्तेर्द्रव्यं कारणम् ॥ ४ ॥

guṇakarmasu sannikṛṣṭeṣu jñānaniṣpatterdravyaṁ kāraṇam ॥4 ॥

Cognition of *guṇas* and *karmas* in close contact (with the sense-organs) should be considered as caused by *dravya*.

[317] सामान्यविशेषेषु सामान्यविशेषाभावात् ततएव ज्ञानम् ॥ ५ ॥

sāmānyaviśeṣeṣu sāmānyaviśeṣābhāvāt tataeva jñānam ॥5 ॥

As *sāmānya* and *viśeṣa* do not exist in *sāmānya* and *viśeṣa* thus their cognition.

[318] सामान्यविशेषापेक्षं द्रव्यगुणकर्मसु ॥ ६ ॥

sāmānyaviśeṣāpekṣaṁ dravyaguṇa-karmasu ॥6 ॥

(Cognition of) *dravya, guṇa* and *karma* presupposes the *sāmānya* and the *viśeṣa.*

[319] द्रव्ये द्रव्यगुणकर्मापेक्षम् ॥ ७ ॥

dravye dravyaguṇakarmāpekṣam ॥7 ॥

In *dravya* (cognition) presupposes *dravya, guṇa* and *karma.*

[320] गुणकर्मसु गुणकर्माऽभावाद् गुणकर्मापेक्षं न विद्यते ॥ ८ ॥

guṇakarmasu guṇakarmā'bhāvād guṇakarmāpekṣam na vidyate ॥8 ॥

As *guṇa* and *karma* do not exist in *guṇa* and *karma* there is no (cognitive) presupposition of *guṇa* and *karma.*

[321] समवायिनः श्वैत्याच्छ्वैत्य बुद्धेश्च श्वेते बुद्धिः ते एते कार्यकारणभूते ॥ ९ ॥

samavāyinaḥ śvaityācchvaitya buddheśca śvete buddhiḥ te ete kāryakāraṇabhūte ॥9 ॥

If an entity is white which is in contact with *samavāya* and due to the knowledge of whiteness cognition arises in the white entity, the two (being and arising of cognition) stand in relation of cause and effect.

[322] द्रव्येष्वनितरेतकारणाः ॥ १० ॥

dravyeṣvanitaretakāraṇāḥ ॥10 ॥

(Cognition arising in various) *dravyas* are not causes of one another.

[323] कारणाऽयौगपद्यात् कारणाक्रमाच्च घटपटादि बुद्धीनां क्रमो न हेतुफलभावात्॥ ११ ॥

kāraṇā'yaugapadyāt kāraṇākramācca ghaṭapaṭādi buddhīnāṁ kramo na hetphalabhāvāt ॥11 ॥

The non-simultaneous coming into being of cause and the causes being sequential in nature give rise to in the sequence of cognition of pot, cloth, etc., not just as (direct) result of a cause.

अष्टमोऽध्यायः प्रथमाह्निकम् समाप्तम्॥

aṣṭamo'dhyāyaḥ prathamāhnikam samāptam ॥

Thus ends the first *āhnika* of the eighth chapter.

द्वितीय आह्निक – Second Āhnika

Types of Jñāna[64]

[324] अयमेष त्वया कृतं भोजयैनमितिबुद्ध्यपेक्षम्॥ १ ॥

ayameṣa tvayā kṛtaṁ bhojayainamitibuddhyapekṣam ॥1 ॥

This is, that is, you did it, feed him such (cognition is a resultant of) different intellects.

[325] दृष्टेषु भावाददृष्टेश्वभावात्॥ २ ॥

dṛṣṭeṣu bhāvādadṛṣṭeśvabhāvāt ॥2 ॥

(Such expressions) exist in references to objects seen and not in objects unseen.

[326] अर्थ इति द्रव्यगुणकर्मसु॥ ३ ॥

artha iti dravyaguṇakarmasu.

---

64. Cognition, knowledge.

The term *artha*[65] applies to *dravya, guṇa* and *karma.*

[327] द्रव्येषु पञ्चात्मकत्वं प्रतिषिद्धम् ॥ ४ ॥

dravyeṣu pañcātmakatvaṁ pratiṣiddham ॥4 ॥

In *dravya* identity with five elements was denied.

[328] भूयस्त्वाद् गन्धवत्त्वाच्च पृथिवी गन्धज्ञाने प्रकृतिः ॥ ५ ॥

bhūyastvād gandhavattvācca pṛthivī gandhajñāne prakṛtiḥ ॥5 ॥

Being plural and having odour *pṛthvī* is the (material cause for the) cognition of odour (by the nose).

[329] तथापस्तेजोवायुश्च रसरूपस्पर्शज्ञानेऽविशेषात् ॥ ६ ॥

tathāpastejovāyuśca rasarūpasparśajñāne'viśeṣāt ॥6 ॥

Similarly, *āpa, teja* and *vāyu* are the material causes of the organs of taste sight and touch.

अष्टमोऽध्यायः द्वितीयाह्निकम् समाप्तम् ॥

aṣṭamo'dhyāyaḥ dvitīyāhnikam samāptam ॥

Thus ends the second *āhnika* of the eighth chapter.

---

65. Object, substance, meaning.

नवम अध्याय – Ninth Chapter

प्रथम आह्निक – First Āhnika

Types of No-Existence and Their Perception

[330] क्रियागुणव्यवदेशाऽभावात् प्रागऽसत् ॥ १ ॥

kriyāguṇavyavadeśā'bhāvāt prāga'sat ॥1 ॥

In the absence of the interaction of *kriyā* and *guṇas*, before coming into being (an effect is said to be) non-existent.[66]

[331] सदसत् ॥ २ ॥

sadasat ॥2 ॥

Existent (becomes) non-existent.[67]

[332] असतः क्रियागुणव्यपदेशाभावादर्थान्तरम् ॥ ३ ॥

asataḥ kriyāguṇavyapadeśābhāvādarthāntaram ॥3 ॥

In the absence of interaction of *kriyā* and *guṇa* it (existence) is distinct from non-existence.

[333] सच्चासत् ॥ ४ ॥

saccāsat ॥4 ॥

Existent also (is) non-existent.[68]

---

66. Definition of *prāgabhāva*.
67. Definition of *dhvaṁsābhāva*.
68. Definition of *anyonyābhāva*.

[334] यच्चान्यदसदतस्तदसत् ॥ ५ ॥

yaccānyadasadatastadasat ॥5 ॥

And that which is different (from both existence and non-existence) is a non-existence (which will never be in existence).[69]

[335] असदिति भूतप्रत्यक्षाभावात् भूतस्मृतेर्विरोधिप्रत्यक्षवत् ॥ ६ ॥

asaditi bhūtapratyakṣābhāvāt bhūtasmṛtervirodhi-pratyakṣavat ॥6 ॥

Perception of a non-existent thing may also result from non-existence of a past perception and a memory of the past, like the perception of an opposing object.

[336] तथाऽभावे भावप्रत्यक्षत्वाच्च ॥ ७ ॥

tathā'bhāve bhāvapratyakṣatvācca ॥7 ॥

Likewise too from perception of existence is non-existence.

[337] एतेनाघटोऽगौरधर्मश्च व्याख्यातः ॥ ८ ॥

etenāghaṭo'gaurdharmaśca vyākhyātaḥ ॥8 ॥

Hereby the non-pot, non-cow and *adharma* is explained.

[338] अभूतं नास्तीत्यनर्थान्तरम् ॥ ९ ॥

abhūtaṁ nāstītyanarthāntaram ॥9 ॥

There is no difference of meaning between that which has not been and that which is not.

[339] नास्ति घटोगेहे इति सतो घटस्य गेहसंसर्ग प्रतिषेधः ॥ १० ॥

nāsti ghaṭogehe iti sato ghaṭasya gehasaṁsarga pratiṣedhaḥ ॥10 ॥

69. Definition of *atyantābhāva*.

There is no pot in the house in a negation of connection between an existent water-pot and the house.

Perception of Self and Other Substances

[340] आत्मन्यात्ममनसोः संयोगविशेषादात्म प्रत्यक्षम् ॥ ११ ॥

ātmanyātmamanasoḥ saṁyogaviśeṣādātma pratyakṣam ॥11 ॥

Perceptual knowledge of *ātmā* is made possible by a particular conjunction between the *ātmā* and the *mana*.

[341] तथा द्रव्यान्तरेषु प्रत्यक्षम् ॥ १२ ॥

tathā dravyāntareṣu pratyakṣam ॥12 ॥

Like perception of the different *dravya*s.

[342] असमाहितान्तः करणा उपसहृतसमाध्यस्तेषाञ्च ॥ १३ ॥

asamāhitāntaḥ karaṇā upasahr̥tasamādhyasteṣāñca ॥13 ॥

In those whose *mana* is not always meditative and in those whose *samādhi*[70] is consummated there is the perception of *ātmā*.

[343] तत् समवायात्कर्मगुणेषु ॥ १४ ॥

tat samavāyātkarmaguṇeṣu ॥14 ॥

(They also perceive) *karma* and *guṇa* from the coinherence of things.

[344] आत्मसमवायादात्मगुणेषु ॥ १५ ॥

ātmasamavāyādātmaguṇeṣu ॥15 ॥

Ātmā being in a form of co-inherence there is also perception of the *guṇa* of *ātmā*.

70. A state of concentration and contemplation induced by meditation.

नवमोऽध्यायः प्रथमाह्निकम् समाप्तम् ॥

navamo'dhyāyaḥ prathamāhnikam samāptam ॥

The first *āhnika* of ninth chapter ends here.

द्वितीय आह्निक – Second Āhnika

Examination of Anumāna[71]

[345] अस्येदं कार्यं कारणं संयोगि विरोधि समवायि चेति लैंगिकम् ॥ १ ॥

asyedaṁ kāryaṁ kāraṇaṁ saṁyogi virodhi samavāyi ceti laiṅgikam ॥1 ॥

Anything connected with any other thing as effect, cause, in contact, as contrary or as inseparably connected will serve as a mark.

[346] अस्येदं कार्यकारणसम्बन्धश्चावयवाद् भवति ॥ २ ॥

asyedaṁ kāryakāraṇasambandhaścāvayavād bhavati ॥2 ॥

That this is associated to this and the cause and effect are connected such is known by examples.

[347] एतेन शब्दं व्याख्यातम् ॥ ३ ॥

etena śabdaṁ vyākhyātam ॥3 ॥

By this is *śabda* explained.

[348] हेतुरपदेशोलिंग प्रमाणं करणमित्यनर्थान्तरम् ॥ ४ ॥

heturapadeśoliṅga pramāṇaṁ karaṇamityanarthāntaram ॥4 ॥

There is no difference of meaning in argument, reason, mark, evidence and instrument.

[349] अस्येदमिति बुद्ध्यपेक्षितत्वात् ॥ ५ ॥

71. Inferential cognition.

asyedamiti buddhyapekṣitatvāt ॥5॥

(Because) they are implicated in the notion of belonging to that (*śabda*).

Examination of Smṛti[72]

[350] आत्ममनसोः संयोगविशेषात् संस्काराच्च स्मृतिः ॥ ६ ॥

ātmamanasoḥ saṁyogaviśeṣāt saṁskārācca smṛtiḥ ॥6॥

Smṛti results from the particular conjunction of the *ātmā* with the *mana* and from *saṁskāra*.[73]

[351] तथा स्वप्नः ॥ ७ ॥

tathā svapnaḥ ॥7॥

So too, dreams (result from conjunction of *ātmā* and *mana*).

[352] स्वप्नान्तिकम् ॥ ८ ॥

svapnāntikam ॥8॥

So too, consciousness in dreams.

[353] धर्माच्च ॥ ९ ॥

dharmācca ॥9॥

And also from *dharma*.

Enumeration of Avidya[74]

[354] इन्द्रियदोषात् संस्कारदोषाच्चाऽविद्या ॥ १० ॥

indriyadoṣāt saṁskāradoṣāccā'vidyā ॥10॥

Ignorance results from the *doṣa* of the organs of

72. Memory.
73. Subliminal impression that fluctuations of the *citta* (which is one of the three of the cognizing apparatus) leaves on it. Other meaning, cf. note 44.
74. Ignorance, nescience.

sense and from the *doṣa* of *saṁskāra*.

[355] तद् दुष्टज्ञानम् ॥ ११ ॥

tad duṣṭajñānam ॥11 ॥

That (*avidyā*) is imperfect cognition.

[356] अदुष्टं विद्या ॥ १२ ॥

aduṣṭaṁ vidyā ॥12 ॥

Free from imperfection is knowledge.

[357] आर्षं सिद्धदर्शनञ्च धर्मेभ्यः ॥ १३ ॥

ārṣaṁ siddhadarśanañca dharmebhyaḥ ॥13 ॥

Knowledge of seers and the perfect vision results from *dharma*.

नवमोऽध्यायः द्वितीयाह्निकम् समाप्तम् ॥

navamo'dhyāyaḥ dvitīyāhnikam samāptam ॥

Here ends the second *āhnika* of the ninth chapter.

दशम अध्याय – Tenth Chapter

प्रथम आह्निक – First Āhnika

Examination of Sukha and Duḥkha

[358] इष्टनिष्टकारणविशेषाद् विरोधाच्च मिथः सुख दुःखयोरर्थान्तरभावः ॥ १ ॥

iṣṭaniṣṭakāraṇaviśeṣād virodhācca mithaḥ sukha duḥkhayorarthāntarabhāvaḥ ॥1 ॥

Due to the difference between desirable and undesirable causes and by opposition *sukha* and *duḥkha* are different in their being.

[359] संशयनिर्णयान्तराभावश्चज्ञानान्तरत्वे ॥ २ ॥

saṁśayanirṇayāntarābhāvaścajñānāntaratve ॥2 ॥

By their non-inclusion of doubt and assurance they are different from cognition.

[360] तयोर्निष्पत्तिः प्रत्यक्षलैंगिकाभ्याम् ॥ ३ ॥

tayorniṣpattiḥ pratyakṣalaiṅgikābhyām ॥3 ॥

The production of them (doubt and assurance) is by means of perception and inference.

[361] अभूदियपि ॥ ४ ॥

abhūdiyapi ॥4 ॥

The notion of the past too (is a difference between the cognition of *sukha* and *duḥkha*.

[362] सति च कार्यदर्शनात् ॥ ५ ॥

sati ca kāryadarśanāt ॥5 ॥

And the effect (of such cognition) is not always observed.

[363] एकार्थसमवायिकारणान्तरेषु दृष्टत्वात् ॥ ६ ॥

ekārthasamavāyikāraṇāntareṣu dṛṣṭavāt ॥6 ॥

(Because *sukha* and *duḥkha*) and observed to coinhere with the same object.

[364] एकदेशे इत्येकस्मिन् शिरः पृष्ठमुदरं मर्माणि तद्विशेषस्तद्विशेषेभ्यः ॥ ७ ॥

ekadeśe ityekasmin śiraḥ pṛṣṭhamudaraṁ marmāṇi tadviśeṣastadviśeṣebhyaḥ ॥7 ॥

The head, the back, the stomach and the vitals are in one (body) but their particularity results from the particularity (of their causes).

दशमोऽध्यायः प्रथमाह्निकम् समाप्तम् ॥

daśamo'dhyāyaḥ prathamāhnikam samāptam ॥

Here ends the first *āhnika* of the tenth chapter.

द्वितीय आह्निक – Second Āhnika

Examination of Cause

[365] कारणमिति द्रव्ये कार्यसमवायात् ॥ १ ॥

kāraṇamiti dravye kāryasamavāyāt ॥1 ॥

That it is a cause, (this position) with regard to *dravya* (rerults) from the co-inherence of effects.

[366] संयोगाद् वा ॥ २ ॥

saṁyogād vā ॥2 ॥

Or from conjunction.

[367] कारणे समवायात् कर्माणि ॥ ३ ॥

kāraṇe samavāyāt karmāṇi ॥3 ॥

Co-inherence in cause results in (non-coinherence in) *karma*.

[368] तथा रूपे कारणैकार्थसमवायाच्च ॥ ४ ॥

tathā rūpe kārṇaikārthasamavāyācca ॥4 ॥

Similarly colour (results from) co-inherence of the cause in the object.

[369] कारणसमवायात् संयोगः पटस्य ॥ ५ ॥

kāraṇasamavāyāt saṁyogaḥ paṭasya ॥5 ॥

Conjunction of cloth due to the co-inherence of cause (is a non-coinherent cause).

[370] कारणकारणसमवायाच्च ॥ ६ ॥

kāraṇakāraṇasamavāyācca ॥6 ॥

Causation of contact also results from the co-inherence of cause in cause.

[371] संयुक्तसमवायादग्नेर्वैशेषिकम् ॥ ७ ॥

saṁyuktasamavāyādagnervaiśeṣikam ॥7 ॥

(Because of) conjunct co-inherence there is a special feature of fire (heat).

Authoritativeness of the Vedas

[372] दृष्टानां दृष्टप्रयोजनानां दृष्टाभावे प्रयोगोभ्युदयाय ॥ ८ ॥

dṛṣṭānāṁ dṛṣṭaprayojanānāṁ dṛṣṭābhāve prayogo'-bhudayāya ॥8 ॥

Observances (according to the injunction of the scriptures) and those (*karmas*) that are seen since they have no visible effects are the cause of prosperity.

...

[373] तद्वचनादाम्नायस्य प्रामाण्यमिति ॥ ९ ॥

tadvacanādāmnāyasya prāmāṇyamiti ॥9 ॥

Authoritativeness pertains to the teaching/tradition/collection since it is a declaration of that.

दशमोऽध्यायः द्वितीयाह्निकम् समाप्तम् ॥

daśamo'dhyāyaḥ dvitīyāhnikam samāptam ॥

Here ends the second *āhnika* of the tenth chapter.

वैशेषिक दर्शनं सम्पूर्णम् ॥

vaiśeṣika darśanaṁ sampūrṇam ॥

Thus Vaiśeṣika philosophy is completed.

Bibliography

Chatterjee, Satischandra and Dhirendra Datta, *An Introduction to Indian Philosophy*, Calcutta, 1984.

Cowell, E.B. and A.E. Gough (trans.). *The Sarva Darśana Saṁgraha by Madhava Ācārya*, The Chowkhamba Sanskrit Series Studies. Vol.X, Varanasi, 1961.

Dasgupta, S.N., *A History of Indian Philosophy*, Vol. 1, Delhi, 1922.

Hiriyanna, M., *The Essentials of Indian Philosophy*, London, 1949.

———, *Outlines of Indian Philosophy*, London, 1968.

Perrett, Roy W. (ed.), *Indian Philosophy: A Collection of Readings*, New York. 2000.

Radhakrishnan, Sarvepalli, *Indian Philosophy*, Vol.II, New York, 1977.

Radhakrishnan, Sarvepalli and Charles A. Moore (eds.), *A Source Book in Indian Philosophy*, Princeton, New Jersey, 1957.

Radhakrishnan, Sarvepalli and board (eds.), *History of Philosophy Eastern and Western*, Vol. I, London, 1967.

Sharma, Jnanchandra, *Vaiśeṣika Sūtra*, New Delhi.

Sharma, Sriram, *Vaiśeṣika Darśana*, Bareilly, 1990.

———, *Nyāya Darśana*, Bareilly, 1990.

———, *Mīmāṁsā Darśana*, Bareilly, 1990.

———, *Sāṁkhya Darśana*, Bareilly, 1990.

Thapar, Romila, 'Sacrifice, surplus and the soul', *History of Religions*, Vol. 33 No. 4, Frank, E. Reynolds, Wendy Doniger, Gary, L. Ebersole, Bruce Lincoln (eds.), Chicago, 1996.

Potter, Karl. H., 'Introduction', *Encyclopedia of Indian Philosophies: Indian Metaphysics and Epistemology: The Tradition of Nyāya-Vaiśeṣika up to Gaṅgeśa*, Delhi, 1997.

Index

AN alphabetical arrangement of Sanskrit technical terms retained in the translation, showing the overall, continuous *sūtra* number (appeared in the parenthesis [ ] before every Sanskrit *śloka*) and continuous foot-note numbers, to be checked for their approximate meanings.